ENGLISH
REPAIR KIT

D1321705

ANGELA BURT
WILLIAM VANDYCK

Illustrated by David Farris

*Hodder
Children's
Books*

a division of Hodder Headline Limited

This edition of *Spelling Repair Kit, Punctuation Repair Kit* and *Grammar Repair Kit* first published by Hodder Children's Books 2001.

Cover illustration by Mark Duffin

Spelling Repair Kit first published as a single volume in Great Britain in 1997 by Hodder Children's Books.

Text copyright © 1997 William Vandyck and Angela Burt
Illustrations copyright © 1997 David Farris

ISBN 0 340 79223 X

A Catalogue record for this book is available from the British Library.

Printed and bound in Great Britain by Clays Ltd, St Ives plc

The paper and board used in this paperback by Hodder Children's Books are natural recyclable products made from wood grown in sustainable forests. The manufacturing processes conform to the environmental regulations of the country of origin.

Hodder Children's Books
A division of Hodder Headline Limited
338 Euston Road
London NW1 3BH

SPELLING REPAIR KIT

WILLIAM VANDYCK
ANGELA BURT

Illustrated by David Farris

a division of Hodder Headline Limited

To the fabulous Elis Stanley Vandyck. Elis has one "l", Vandyck is all one word and d-y-<u>c</u>-k, and fabulous is as fabulous does.
With tons of love, Dad

For John with affection and gratitude
Angela

CONTENTS

INTRODUCTION

Why not to buy this book

There are two reasons which people give for not bothering to learn to spell properly. They usually say either something like:

1. You don't really need to know how to spell.

So long as you get close, people know what you mean — and anyway all computers have spellchecks, these days, innit?

OR

2. You can't learn how to spell.

You either can or you can't. Luckily I was born a brilliant speller.

CLEVER
TROUSERS

There are just two things to remember about these two points.

THEY ARE BIG FAT LIES.

Big Fat Lie One: "You don't really need to know how to spell".

This really is rubbish. **STUPID**
Question: Do you want to look **STUPID** ?
No, we didn't think so. Well, here are two facts then.

Remember, they're just facts, OK? Just accept it.

FACT 1 — The DAILY FACTS — Spelling Matters A Lot Says Everyone

FACT 2 — The Other Daily Facts — And They're Right

And we can prove it.

Look. Imagine you're an examiner, or an employer, or a friend reading one of these notes. Which one makes you think the writer is stupid?

I left my home in 1997 to do great things

I left ~~me~~ mi ~~me~~ hom in 19~~9~~97 ~~te~~ to do grate ~~heis~~ things

Clue: It's this one

If you've got a computer, you might think the spellcheck would solve all your problems – but you'd be wrong!

Spellchecks can only correct words if they're very nearly right anyway. And they can't pick out wrong spellings which would be right spellings if you meant something else. So, if you wrote "pane" (of glass) when you meant "pain" (in the . . . neck), it wouldn't correct you. It wouldn't pick up the "grate" in the note above. And anyway, if you haven't learnt to spell, what do you do when you haven't got the computer readily available. Look

STUPID ?

And if you thought spelling didn't matter, or that spellchecks would spot all mistakes, look:

You are invited to come hunting bear.

You are invited to come hunting bare.

The spellcheck wouldn't have picked that out, would it?

And you might think the difference mattered just a teeny bit, no?

Big Fat Lie Two: "You can't learn how to spell".

This really is rubbish, too. Again, we can prove it. This time, we can prove it through completely independent research.

We took fifteen people and one 1-week old baby called Elis. We set them all *exactly* the same spelling test, so that there was no unfairness.

The lad Elis didn't come first. Can you guess the reason why?

The *only* reason for this is - obviously - that Elis had not by the time of this test had a chance to learn how to spell.

See?

It's not just that you *can* learn how to spell - you *have* to. It's the only way.

Now, there's some good news. And some better news. And then some best news.

The GOOD news

is that in order to spell, you don't have to learn a dictionary. It's all a bit bewildering when you think of how many words there are (at the last count, absolutely tons). But the thing is, if you remember a few tricks (or "rules"), you'll be able to spell an enormous number of words.

So you don't have to be like:

Una the Unnecessary Worker

You can be like:

Stanley Savenergy

And now . . .

The BETTER news.

We'll muck about a bit along the way. So, watch this space:

General Malaise

Okay, you can stop watching the space now. Carry on.

For example, for no reason at all we're suddenly going to write:

The VEST.

Oh, all right, there is a bit of a reason for it. The word "vest" sounds like "best". And the best news is yet to come. PTO. (That is not POT misspelt. Or TOP misspelt. Or even TPO misspelt. It means "Please Turn Over".)

The BEST news is that you won't have to battle through this alone. You're going to be helped by the garage mechanics, who are:

Say hello, Zelda:

Oh dear. See if you can work out how Steven got his name.

There'll be a few other people dropping in along the way, too. But right now, let's go to work.

MORE THAN ONE

What's wrong with this note?

GIVE ME ALL YOUR BOXS OF SWEETES OR I'LL SMACK YOU IN YOUR TOOTHS WITH WET CODS

Well, for a start it's not very polite, is it?

But more importantly it looks very stupid because the spelling is all wrong for the plurals.

A plural is a word which refers to more than one thing. So, the plural of "pen" is "pens".

Now, yes, it can be quite tricky making some nouns plural. There are some words that, frankly, act a bit weird when they go from singular (one) to plural. We're just about to have a look at those.

A noun is a word that names —"identifies"— a thing, like car, spanner, repair, or terror!

But don't despair.

There is some slightly good news coming.

And then, there is some tremendously fabulous better news.

Hang on in there.

13

OK, here are some of the weird words.

Singular	Plural
one mouse	three mice
one tooth	five teeth
one woman	six women
one child	two children
one goose	four geese

Loopy. Mad. Sorry.

Then some words are weird because they don't change at all.
They're exactly the same in the singular and in the plural.

one sheep	two sheep
one moose	five moose
one cod	three cod

Some words go to the other extreme and have *two* plurals.

appendix	appendixes
	appendices
memorandum	memorandums
	memoranda
syllabus	syllabuses
	syllabi

You should use your dictionary to check exceptional words like
these and if you want to learn them you have to learn each
word individually.

The slightly good news is that you probably know a lot of them
already. And the fabulous news is that you do not need to learn
the plural of every word you know!

 Hundreds of thousands of words follow easy rules (or
patterns). All you have to do with these straightforward
words is to learn the rules they follow, and then you can
spell huge numbers of words correctly.

A (one) sheep.   Two Sheep.   A sheep one-two.

Mr Clevertrousers'
Advanced Mental Wandering for Curious Fools

Remember, you do not need to remember anything in this box - even this bit.

Some words have weird endings because of Latin. They're Latin words, and people just sort of got so into the habit of using the Latin version of the plural that they forgot to stop doing it when we started speaking English. You will come across some words that end in -um, for which the Latin plural was -a. More than one memorandum? They'd say memoranda.

Now, some people will tell you that Latin is terribly important, educates your mind, blah blah blah.

Well, if it's so cool, how come the people who go on about it are so boring, eh?

And remember –

syllabuses (the areas covered by courses or exams) should on no account be confused with the dreaded:

silly buses.

Some of the rules you probably half-know already. You've just got to be confident enough to use them safely every time.

Take these two words, **chair** and **box**, for instance.

    one chair three chair**s**
    one box   two box**es**

How do you know whether to add **–s** or **–es** without having to learn each word individually?

There's a very easy answer.

You can always HEAR when you have to add -es because you are adding an extra syllable.

Say to yourself:
    chair   chair**s**
    box   box**es**.

Can you HEAR the extra syllable when you say "box-**es**"?

Here are some words to say aloud. Count the syllables as you say them.

    punch   punch**es**
    witch   witch**es**
    bus   bus**es**

And look, it works for words which start with more than one syllable, too.

    actress   actress**es**
    princess   princess**es**
    witness   witness**es**   no extra syllable - not es!
    elephant   elephant**s**

You can see that if you add -es to a word of one syllable, you end up with two syllables. If you add -es to a word of two syllables, you end up with three syllables, and so on.

You've now learned two important spelling rules.

Syllable. Syllable. Hmm. Is that a type of pudding?

No, are you thinking of "syllabub", a dish made of cream or milk curdled with wine or similar, and sometimes solidified with gelatin?

Er, no, I remember which pudding I was thinking of... treacle tart.

Right. Well, the number of syllables in a word is the number of sounds in that word. So, "hat" has one syllable. "Thumps" has one but "punches" has two. "Zelda" has two. "Steven" has two, too.

Like this.

No, Steven, that's "Steven has a tutu". What I'm saying is that the word "Steven" has two syllables. But not, it seems, two brain cells. Let's see if anyone can do better than Steven. Can you say how many syllables there are in these?

Towns
Catapult
Pointy
"Help me, I'm stuck," said the man with the pointy head who had landed upside down.

Answers: 1, 3, 2, 19.

Remember now:

"Trou - ser"

2 Syllables.

2 Silly bulls[1].

No worries!

Worry...

---

[1] And now you know another difference between silly bul**ls** and silly bus**es**. Clever, eh?

Rule 1

You make most words plural by adding **-s**.

Rule 2

You make some words plural by adding **-es** when you can *hear* that you need an extra syllable.

Why not simply say that words ending in sibilants require **-es** in the plural?

Well, yes. That's another way of putting it but then I'd have to explain that sibilants are hissing sounds like -s, -x, -z, -ch, -tch, and -sh. I will if you like. There, I've done it.

Now everyone can be clevertrousers.

Rule 2   Pointlessly clever version.

Words ending in sibilants require -es in the plural

which are hissing sounds like -s,-x,-ch, -tch and -sh

It's time for an MOT! (That's a **M**iserable **O**ld **T**est.) Test your understanding of these two rules by completing the following:

BASIC MOT

1.	one book	two book____
2.	one wish	three wish____
3.	one teacher	four teacher____
4.	one pen	five pen____
5.	one glass	six glass____

The answers for all the tests are at the back of the book. Check yours before going on to the advanced MOT. Make sure that you understand exactly when you need to add -es and when you need just to add -s.

The advanced MOT may look hard because you may not have met all of the words before. Don't worry if any words are unfamiliar. We've deliberately put some hard words in to prove to you that you can apply the rules with absolute confidence and get the right answer every time.

ADVANCED MOT

1. winch____

2. ruminant____

3. blemish____

4. mnemonic____

5. zygoranismagicianisticalist_____ – see, you can even do it for words that don't exist.

Next we're going to look at how to form the plural of nouns ending in -y, like fairy, boy and party. Now, the important thing to remember is that it all depends on whether the word ends in a *vowel* + y, or a *consonant* + y.

What's a VOWEL?
What's a CONSONANT?

A, E, I, O, U are vowels. The rest of the letters of the alphabet are consonants.

Here comes Rule 3. It's wonderful because there are no exceptions at all. All the nouns in the English language which end in -y follow this rule.

Rule 3 Add **-s** to words ending in a vowel + y. Change y to i and add **-es** with words ending in a consonant + y.

Have a look at some examples.

examples of vowel + y

boy	boys
chimney	chimneys
monkey	monkeys
alley	alleys
day	days
guy	guys

examples of consonant + y

city	cities
party	parties
fairy	fairies
gipsy	gipsies
estuary	estuaries

Those vowels in full: **A E I O U**

Mr Clevertrousers' VALUE-FREE Information Spot

Did you know that the shortest word in the English language using all the vowels in alphabetical order is "f<u>a</u>c<u>e</u>t<u>i</u><u>ou</u>s"?

How about the time I hit my head on a biscuit and said "Aeiou!"

That doesn't count.

Here's one way of remembering that the vowels are AEIOU. Think of this picture and remember:

"An Entertaining Idiot Often Undresses"

Would you like to check *your* skills now? You will do just as well if you follow the rule carefully. In fact, if you follow the rule carefully, you *can't* make a mistake.

Just look at the last two letters. You have to know whether the word ends with a vowel + y or a consonant + y.

BASIC MOT

Make these words plural.

1. fly
2. toy
3. bully
4. holiday
5. donkey
6. berry
7. spy
8. story
9. valley
10. pony

I like rules which don't have any exceptions. I hope there are no exceptions to the next rule as well.

There are a few but nothing to worry about. You just have to say the words aloud and you'll know how to spell them.

Are you ready for the advanced MOT now? We've chosen long words that you may not know just to make the test look very difficult. As you know, you've just got to see whether the word ends in a vowel + y or a consonant + y to know how to form the plural correctly every time.

ADVANCED MOT

Make these words plural.

1. essay
2. fantasy
3. opportunity
4. factory
5. volley

6. university
7. quality
8. pulley
9. responsibility
10. convoy

Find out how well you did by checking your answers with the answers at the end of the book.

The next rule applies to nouns ending in -f and -fe.

Rule 4 Add **-s** to form the plural of words ending in **-f** or **-fe**.

In just a few words the f changes to v or ve in the plural. You can always HEAR when this happens: cal**ves**, hal**ves**, wi**ves**, li**ves**, thie**ves**, lea**ves**, and so on.

You don't need a sheaf of paper – use your loaf!   *You don't need sheaves of paper – use your loaves!*

So, what's the plural of "The White Cliff of Dover"?

Well, say the plural of "cliff" to yourself. It keeps the "f" sound, doesn't it? So, the plural of "cliff" is "cliffs".

And look how stupid you'd look if you wrote the wrong thing:

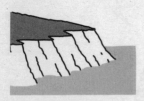   

A. The White Cliffs of Dover.   **B. The White Clives of Dover.**

There's just one more rule we have to consider and that's the one for forming the plural of nouns ending in **-o**.

Before you turn the page, how many words can you think of that end in -o?

ODD ONE OUT

Which is the ONE word in this list which has a **v** sound in the plural?

giraffe
café
sheriff
shelf
cliff

Say them aloud and you'll hear the answer...

The answer is at the end of the book.

The Importance of Spelling Through the Ages, part 247

What is the plural of "wife"?

It was always very important to be able to show the difference between:

The Six Wives of Henry VIII

and

The Six Whiffs of Henry VIII.

Words ending in **o**

Here are some:

piano	**banjo**	**soprano**	**contralto**	**photo**
disco	**rodeo**	**sombrero**	**cuckoo**	**kangaroo.**

Rule 5

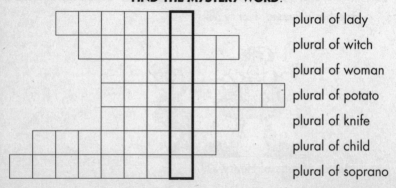

Add **-s** to form the plural of words ending in -o.

No exceptionos, I hope!

Just listen carefully.

There are just a few exceptions. That's why we've left this rule to the last in this chapter. There are two ways of tackling the exceptions. Choose whichever method suits you best.

Method 1: Use a dictionary. If you have to add -es in the plural because the word is an exception to the rule, the dictionary will remind you. If you just have to add -s, the dictionary won't bother to mention it.

Method 2: Learn the most important exceptions (the words that you're most likely to need) and just check the ones you're not certain about.

Learn: **cargoes   dominoes   echoes   heroes   mosquitoes potatoes   tomatoes   tornadoes   torpedoes   volcanoes**

Perhaps you'd like to practise all that you have learned and
FIND THE MYSTERY WORD.

plural of lady

plural of witch

plural of woman

plural of potato

plural of knife

plural of child

plural of soprano

Just Mucking About

Do you know about palindromes?

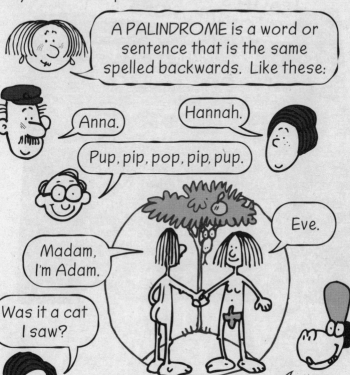

A PALINDROME is a word or sentence that is the same spelled backwards. Like these:

Anna.

Hannah.

Pup, pip, pop, pip, pup.

Eve.

Madam, I'm Adam.

Was it a cat I saw?

How about this - siht tuoba woh.

Can you think of any? Do remember not to confuse:

1. a palindrome: **Eve**

with

2. a pally dromedary!

Will you be my friend?

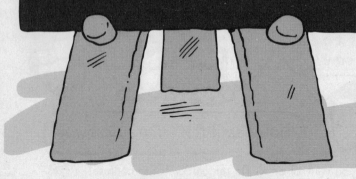

COLIN'S CHALKBOARD CONCLUSIONS

PLURALS

1. Generally add -s.
2. Add -es if you can hear the extra syllable (eg boxes).
3. If a word ends consonant + y change the y to i and add -es, eg city, cities.
4. For words ending -f or -fe, change the -f or -fe to -v or -ve if you can hear that's what happens.
5. There are exceptions, including some mad ones. Try to learn the most common ones.

So, if you had me and _another_ Colin here, Zelda, what would you say?

I'm twice as bored by you.

ADDING ENDINGS

Normally there's no problem when you add an ending to one word to make another one. You just join the ending on and that's that.

clean + **er** = cleaner
paint + **ing** = painting
play + **ful** = playful
astonish + **ment** = astonishment
trouble + **some** = troublesome
special + **ity** = speciality

Why not call these things by their proper name? They're suffixes. Everyone knows that!

CLEVER TROUSERS

It really doesn't matter whether you call them endings or suffixes.

I can give you a wonderful tip. Whenever you add "full" to a word, it ALWAYS becomes -ful.

Now that's what I call a use**ful** comment. I hope our boast**ful** friend is playing care**ful** attention to your help**ful** advice, Zelda.

Our next rule is about adding endings to -y words. It's the ones ending in a consonant + y that need special care.

Rule 6

Just add the ending if the word ends in a vowel + y.

play + ful = playful
play + ing = playing

BUT

Take care if the word ends in a consonant + y.
Change the y to i before adding the ending.

beauty + ful = beautiful
copy + ed = copied

(But keep the y before -ing: copying.)

SUPPLY THE VITAL MISSING LETTER!

1. enjoy + ment = enjo _ ment
2. cry + ed = cr _ ed
3. pay + ing = pa _ ing
4. early + er = earl _ er
5. empty + ness = empt _ ness

Don't forget the exceptions –
said, paid, laid, and daily.

SOPHIE
SMARTIPANTS

Are you ready to try the advanced MOT?

Just remember:

play + ful = playful
beauty + ful = beautiful.

These will help you
to remember the rule.

We have deliberately tried to make the advanced MOT look very hard by putting in some words that you may never have tried to spell before. Just apply the rule and you'll supply the correct missing letter every time.

ADVANCED MOT

(It's not so difficult as it looks!)

Supply the vital missing letter:

1.	lonely + ness	=	lonel _ ness
2.	mercy + ful	=	merc _ ful
3.	portray + al	=	portra _ al
4.	melody + ous	=	melod _ ous
5.	annoy + ance	=	anno _ ance
6.	envy + able	=	env _ able
7.	employ + er	=	emplo _ er
8.	marry + age	=	marr _ age
9.	luxury + ous	=	luxur _ ous
10.	pity + less	=	pit _ less

Our next rule concerns words ending in silent **-e**.

You may already have had some problems with these words, wondering whether to keep the -e or drop it when you add an ending.

The secret is this:

Check whether the ending is a vowel suffix (an ending beginning with a, e, i, o, u, for example "ing") or a consonant suffix (an ending beginning with a consonant, for example "ful").

Rule 7

Drop the -e when you add a vowel suffix.
(Mak**e** + ing = ma<u>k</u>ing)

Keep the -e when you add a consonant suffix.
(Car**e** + ful = car<u>ef</u>ul)

Remember that -y counts as a vowel suffix when it sounds like -e: scare + y = scary.

It's worth learning five exceptions to the silent -e rule: truly, awful, ninth, argument, wisdom. You'd expect these words to keep the -e and they don't.

Sophie Smartypants has made three mistakes in her homework (hooray!). Be her teacher and mark her answers for her and write in the corrections for her to learn.

1.	love + ing	loving
2.	care + less	carless
3.	laze + y	lazy
4.	sincere + ly	sincerly
5.	safe + ty	saftey

As a result of being careless, I am now carless

Henry VIII needs help adding endings to silent -e words. He has been too lazy (laze + y) to learn the rule in the past. Now he's written a letter to Jane Seymour and needs help with five words. Could you look at this list and write the words he needs in the right spaces?

definite + ly   **lone + ly**   **grate + ful**
write + ing   **hope + ing**   **sincere + ly**

Dear Jane,
    I am _____ because I am so _____ since Anne Boleyn's head came clean off. Both my hired killers (Og and Stig) agree that it was _____ an accident. Or "Axe"-ident, more like, heh heh heh.
    Anyway, I was _____ you might be free next week. Or n-axe-d week says Stig. Heh heh. I would be _____ for a prompt reply.

                                    Yours _____,
                                    Henry VIII

PS: PBAAxe.

Now let's look at the 1-1-1 rule. This rule tells you whether you've got to double a letter or not.

First of all, try to guess why the rule is called 1-1-1.

Find *three* ways in which these words are alike.

fit   spot   sin   drop   flat

Could you find the three ways?

1. They are all words of ONE syllable.
2. They all end with just ONE consonant.
3. They all have ONE vowel in the middle.

Calling it the 1-1-1 rule helps to remind you that the word has to fit the rule in three ways.

REMEMBER the rule does NOT apply to a word like **crash** because this ends in *two* consonants.

REMEMBER the rule does NOT apply to a word like **cool** because that has *two* vowels in the middle.

Now let's see what happens when you add vowel suffixes and consonant suffixes to 1-1-1 words.

Better still, see if you can work out the rule for yourself.

fit + ness = fitness	fit + est = fittest
spot + less = spotless	spot + ed = spotted
sin + ful = sinful	sin + er = sinner
drop + let = droplet	drop + ing = dropping
flat + ly = flatly	flat + en = flatten

Could you work out the rule?

Rule 8

NO CHANGE to a 1-1-1 word if you add a consonant suffix.
DOUBLE the last letter of a 1-1-1 word if you add a vowel suffix.

There's only one 1-1-1 rule
One 1-1-1 rule
And it's "No change to a 1-1-1 word for consonant suffixes, but double the last letter for vowel suffixes".

Which is the right spelling of the following not-at-all well known sayings?

1. The weather today will be hot and funy/funny.

2. Survival of the fatest/fattest.

Answers: funny, fattest

COLIN'S CHALKBOARD CONCLUSIONS

ADDING AN ENDING

1. Full is always "ful" as an ending.
2. (i) Vowel + y – add the ending
   (but said, paid, laid, daily).
   (ii) Consonant + y – change y to i before adding
   the ending.
3. If a word ends in a silent -e:
   (i) drop it for a vowel suffix (treating y as a
   vowel here) eg make + ing = making.
   (ii) keep it for a consonant suffix
   eg care + ful = careful.
4. No change to a 1 – 1 – 1 word for consonant
   suffixes; double the last letter for vowel suffixes.

Ahhh, I like happy endings.

What, like
"And then Colin
got strung up"?

HOMOPHONES

Do you know what a homophone is? Homophones are groups of words which *sound* the same but which are spelled differently.

Here are some examples of homophones. You may know a lot of others.

blue and **blew**
weak and **week**
rain, **rein** and **reign**
pour, **paw** and **pore**

"Homophone" means same sound:
homo (same) + phone (sound).
More old language.

It is important to choose the right word for the situation because otherwise you risk confusing your reader.

For example, do you think this jar of face cream is going to be a big seller?

NULIFE
cleans your paws
while you sleep

I meant for anyone except Steven.

There are hundreds of homophones in the English language. Most of them cause no trouble at all once you've got used to them. Some are more tricky.

Test how many you know in the puzzles that follow.

MISSING PARTNERS

Spell the missing partner. The first one has been done for you.

four	f o r
hole	_ _ _ _ _
tail	_ _ _ _
throne	_ _ _ _ _ _
wood	_ _ _ _ _
sun	_ _ _

Now use your answers to complete this newspaper item:

Bob's ____ was ____ out of school ___ eating the _____ school's food by himself. He told some ____ about getting into the Guinness Book of Records, but then he ____ , wouldn't he?

This section is very difficult. See how many missing partners you know.

prophet	_ _ _ _ _ _
aisle	_ _ _ _
medal	_ _ _ _ _ _
him	_ _ _ _
ceiling	_ _ _ _ _ _ _

IT IS OF COURSE IMPORTANT TO BE ABLE TO WRITE THE DIFFERENCE BETWEEN:

BRIGHTER THAN A THOUSAND SUNS

AND

BRIGHTER THAN A THOUSAND SONS.

MISSING PAIRS

Use these clues to find the missing pairs. The first one has been done for you.

a small hole that allows water to run out   l e a k
a vegetable belonging to the onion family   l e e k

opposite of female
letters and parcels sent through the post   _ _ _ _

to come to the end of life
to colour clothes permanently   _ _ _

the back part of the foot
to become cured   _ _ _ _

to change
the table used in church for the
Communion service   _ _ _ _ _

Dictionary Quiz

Use your dictionary (if you wish) to find out the difference in meaning between these pairs.

serial   cereal   berth   birth

stationery   stationary   yoke   yolk

border   boarder

Cereal Killer

39

Zandra has written a nice friendly letter to Percy but she has chosen the wrong homophone *ten times*. Can you spot the mistakes?

7 Seaview Road,
Brightling,
Devon.

Monday, 10th June

Deer Percy,

Wood yew like to come to stay with us for a hole weak? We can go to the beech every day and have a grate time.

Please right back soon and say yes.

With love,
Zandra

P.S. I hope yew can reed this!

MISSING LETTERS

Can you find the homophone and fill in the missing letters?

soul	s o l e
horse	h _ _ _ _ e
sum	s _ _ e
meet	m _ _ t
aloud	a _ _ _ _ _ d
check	c _ _ _ _ e

Next follows a checklist of everyday homophones that cause a lot of trouble. The examples should help you always choose the right word when you need it.

CHECKLIST

hear	Can you **hear** that noise?
here	Stay **here** and wait a moment.
it's	**It's** been raining all day. (= it has)
its	**Its** tail is twitching.
its	**It's** alive! (= it is).
knew	I **knew** your old grandmother.
new	I prefer the **new** one.
know	I **know** your girlfriend.
no	I have **no** idea why she is called "Psycho".
passed	She has **passed** her exam.
past	They walked straight **past** us.
	The **past** is over and done with.
	Do you know the **past** tense of "go"?
their	**Their** cat is missing.
there	I'll wait for you over **there**.
they're	**They're** coming home today.
	(= they are)
to	We are going **to** Dublin.
	I'd like **to** help you.
too	He is **too** lazy. (= excessively)
	Are you coming **too**? (= as well)
two	You can have **two** cakes each. (= 2)
who's	**Who's** been eating my sweets? (= who has)
who's	**Who's** coming with me? (= who is)
whose	**Whose** grandmother is this?
	The people **whose** cat is missing are very upset.

Hear, Pussycat!

Hear what?

TESTING, TESTING

Use the checklist to help you choose the missing words in these sentences.

1. _____ coming to your party? (who's/whose)
2. I can _____ every word you say. (hear/here)
3. My cat is ___ lazy ___ catch more than ___ mice. (to/too/two)
4. _____ very windy today. (it's/its)
5. I _____ the answer. It's ___. (know/no)

OK, that's enough of that! Let's have a look at another group of words that can cause a lot of trouble.

WORDS EASILY CONFUSED

These words are not homophones. They don't sound exactly alike but are close enough for people to muddle them up.

Make sure you know how to say them.

Make sure you know which is which.

TRICKY WORDS

bought (from BUY)
I've **bought** you an ice-cream.

brought (from BRING)
I **brought** my spider to school.

breath (rhymes with DEATH)
You can see your **breath** in the air on a cold day.

breathe (rhymes with SNEEZE)
"**Breathe** regularly," says top doctor.

clothes (you wear these)
All my **clothes** are too small.

cloths (do housework with these)
Use soft **cloths** to polish your furniture.

desert (very sandy!)
She was lost in the Sahara **desert** for three days.

dessert (pudding)
We had apple pie for **dessert**.

lightening (making lighter)
We are **lightening** her load as much as we can.

lightning (and thunder)
A loud clap of thunder followed the flash of **lightning**.

loose (not fixed tight)
I have a **loose** tooth.

lose (to stop having)
Don't **lose** this £5 note.

of (sounds like ov)
Would you like a piece **of** cake?

off (hear the F sound)
The thief ran **off**.

quiet (not noisy)
She was as **quiet** as a mouse.

quite (absolutely)
Are you **quite** sure you came from Mars?

were (rhymes with HER)
You **were** standing next to her.

where (rhymes with AIR)
Where you going?

TEST YOUR UNDERSTANDING

bought or brought?   We have _____ a castle haunted by a man who doesn't believe in ghosts.

off or of?   He had dived _____ the castle tower into the moat for a bet.

where or were?   No one had told him _____ the enormous and hungry Moaty Fish _____.

cloths or clothes?   Only his _____ survived.

of or off?   Now he has to haunt the place naked, which really cheeses him _____ .

43

ONE WORD OR TWO?

It can be difficult knowing whether you have to write one word or two on some occasions.

Always one word: **upstairs**
                    downstairs
                    cannot

Always two words: **a lot**
                    in front
                    in fact
                    all right

Sometimes one word; sometimes two words!! It all depends on which meaning you want.

ALMOST (= nearly) **ALL MOST** (= all of us).

I have **almost** finished.
We are **all most** grateful.

ALREADY (= before the expected time) **ALL READY** (= all of us)

We have **already** finished.
We are **all ready** for an emergency.

ALSO (= as well) **ALL SO** (= all of you)

He is **also** an artist.
You are **all so** kind.

ALWAYS (= at all times) **ALL WAYS** (= all the ways)

She is **always** happy.
All ways into the town were blocked by snow.

SOMETIMES (= now and again) **SOME TIMES**

I **sometimes** go fishing.
There are **some times** when I can't think of anything to do.

Just Mucking About

Time to relax! Those who like words and value-free information may be interested in homonyms and homographs.

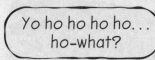

Yo ho ho ho ho. . .
ho-what?

HOMONYMS same spelling
same pronunciation
different meaning

For example, **box** is a homonym. It has at least two meanings:

a **box** of chocolates
to **box** in the boxing ring

Can you think of at least two meanings for each of these homonyms?

faint   **pen**   **plain**   **pine**   **match**

HOMOGRAPHS   same spelling
different pronunciation
different meaning

These are fascinating. See how you can say a homograph in two different ways. First say the word stressing the first syllable and then say the word stressing the second syllable.

project
PROject We are doing a *project* on transport through the ages.
proJECT You must *project* your voice to the back of the hall.

Say each of these words in two ways and see how they can mean two different things. (Look in the Answers section if you get stuck.)

entrance	ENtrance	enTRANCE
permit	PERmit	perMIT
conduct	CONduct	conDUCT
extract	EXtract	exTRACT
refuse	REfuse	reFUSE

COLIN'S CHALKBOARD CONCLUSIONS

Beware of the following:

1. Homophones: same sound, different spelling. Make sure you get the ~~write~~ right one.

2. Words which sound similar eg bought/brought, quiet/quite.

3. One word or two eg almost, all most.

   Tip for 1 - 3: think about the meaning of the word rather than just the sound when you spell it.

4. Homonyms: same spelling, same pronunciation, different meaning.

5. Homographs: same spelling, different pronunciation, different meaning.

4 & 5: A bit of a laugh - and happily no worries for spellers.

Do you want a box?

Ooooh, yes please.

ADDING BEGINNINGS

You have seen how words can be formed by adding endings to what are called "base words". In this section, we see how words can be formed by adding beginnings.

Shall we call them prefixes?

It really doesn't matter whether you call them prefixes or beginnings.

CLEVER TROUSERS

PREFIX THE LEGIONNAIRE ALWAYS CAME FIRST

PREFIX NECK-CRIX MAGIC-TRIX PICK-N-MIX SUFFIX

WHOLE WORD PREFIXES

Sometimes prefixes can be whole words. Some whole word prefixes are: **out**, **over**, **under**, **up**.

Some quite ordinary base words are made into complicated-looking words when prefixes and suffixes are added. These words can look difficult to spell until you see how they are built up.

One of the longest words in the English language is said to be:

ANTIDISESTABLISHMENTARIANISM

It looks impossible to spell (or even say) until you see that it's simply the base word **ESTABLISH** with two prefixes (at the beginning) and three suffixes (at the end). Study the structure and you'll be able to spell it - and say it! - without difficulty.

ANTI   DIS   **ESTABLISH**   MENT   ARIAN   ISM

If you learn how to spell prefixes and suffixes, you're more than halfway to spelling thousands and thousands of "combination" words.

Can you supply the missing letters? The prefix and the first letter of the base word has been given to you to start you off.

OUT

outline	a drawing showing a general shape
outc_____	a person without home or friends
outb_____	a sudden explosion of anger
outl_____	a criminal, a person outside the law
outs_____	the edge of a town

OVER

oversleep	to sleep longer than planned
overc_____	to ask too high a price
overb_____	to lose one's footing and fall over
overf_____	to spill over
overb_____	over the side of a boat

UNDER

underground	below the ground
underw_____	clothes like pants and vests
underl_____	emphasise, draw a line under
underg_____	plants and bushes growing under trees
underh_____	deceitful, sly

UP

uproot	to pull up by the roots, to destroy
ups_____	to cause someone to be unhappy
upr_____	vertical, standing or sitting straight
upr_____	loud and noisy shouting
uph_____	tremendous change or disturbance

Don't worry if the word you make by adding a prefix to a base word ends up with a double letter. That's how it should be!

over + react = over**r**eact
under + rate = under**r**ate

NEGATIVE PREFIXES

Some prefixes make their base words negative.

visible   **in**visible

There are four prefixes (**in**-, **un**-, **dis**-, **mis**-) which can reverse the meaning of base words in this way. The main problem is deciding which one you should use!

1. Remember too that sometimes when you add a negative prefix to a base word you will end up with a double letter in the "combination" word.

u**n** + **n**atural = un**n**atural
di**s** + **s**atisfied = dis**s**atisfied
mi**s** + **s**pell = mis**s**pell

2. Take care when you add in- to some words. Over the centuries, the n has changed to another letter to make the word easier to say.

These special forms need to be learned by heart. Here is a sample. Note other examples as you come across them.

noble	ignoble
legal	illegal
legible	illegible
literate	illiterate
patient	impatient
perfect	imperfect
possible	impossible
regular	irregular
relevant	irrelevant
responsible	irresponsible

You know most of these words already. So don't worry. You'll have to learn only a very few.

TEST YOUR WORD POWER
(and find the mystery word!)

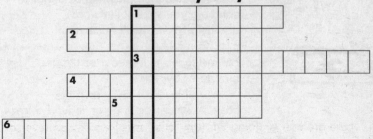

Use the correct negative prefix to form the opposite of:

1. OBEY
2. CORRECT
3. NECESSARY
4. BEHAVE
5. LEGAL
6. PATIENT

Did you find the mystery word?

Note how important prefixes can be:

NUMBER PREFIXES

Understanding the meaning of prefixes can help you spell some words, particularly ones with numbers in.

For instance: is it bipass or bypass, bicycle or bycycle?

Easy. A **by**pass goes by or around a town or city instead of going through it.
(by- means BY.)
A **bi**cycle is a cycle with two wheels.
(bi- means TWO).

There are lots of other prefixes to do with numbers. Here are some of the most common ones.

uni- (one, single):   **uni**corn, **uni**cycle
mono- (one, single):   **mono**rail, **mono**syllable
bi- (two):   **bi**cycle, **bi**focals
tri- (three):   **tri**cycle, **tri**pod
quadr- (quad):   **quadr**uped, **quadr**uplets
deca- (ten):   **deca**de, **dec**imal
cent- (one hundred):   **cent**imetre, **cent**ury
mill- (one thousand):   **mill**imetre, **mill**ennium
poly- (many):   **poly**gon, **poly**syllable
omni- (all):   **omni**bus, **omni**vorous

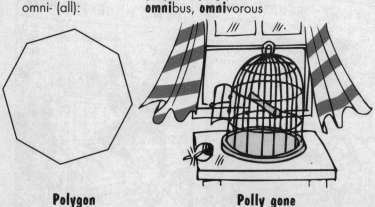

Polygon   **Polly gone**

FIND THE WORDS

All these anagrams can be unscrambled to make words beginning with number prefixes.

Find the prefix first and the rest will follow.

pdeeetnic: This creature has not really got a hundred feet.
dretint: Neptune has one of these three-pronged forks.
thlacendo: To win one of these you would have to get the highest overall score in ten different events.

Just Mucking About Again

Anagrams can be a bit of a laugh in general.

"Dazle" is an anagram of Zelda, which is cool, because I'm a dazzling person.

"Stevne" is an anagram of, er, Steven.

Oh, come on Steven, you can do better than that. You really do make one v. tense.

Why?

Oh, I give up.

Can you make an anagram of your name?

And what anagram is this:

Segg

Answer: Scrambled "Eggs"

53

MORE PREFIXES

Most of the prefixes in the list below have come into our language from Latin and Greek (like the number prefixes we have just looked at). These prefixes can be very hard to spell but, on the other hand, once you HAVE learned how to spell them, you've often learned to spell the hardest part of lots of related words. And, in addition, you will have an important clue to their meaning. Look at the prefix chrono-. It comes from the Greek and means "time". Now a *chronic* illness is simply one that lasts for a long time (often for years). It is not necessarily a serious illness as so many people mistakenly suppose.

chrono- (time), **chron**ic, **chron**icle, **chron**ological, **chron**ology, **chron**ometer

ante- (before): **ante**natal

anti- (against): **anti**septic

auto- (self): **auto**biography

bene- (well): **bene**fit

chrono- (time): **chrono**logical

circum- (around): **circum**ference

contra- (against): **contra**dict

de- (from): **de**part

ex- (out of): **ex**pel

extra- (beyond): **extra**ordinary

fore- (before): **fore**cast

homo- (same): **homo**phone

inter- (between): **inter**national

male- (evil): **male**volent

micro- (small): **micro**scope

photo- (light): **photo**copy

per- (through): **per**forate

post- (after): **post**script

pre- (before): **pre**pare

psycho- (mind, soul): **psycho**logy

re- (again): **re**pay

semi- (half): **semi**-circle

sub- (under): **sub**marine

super- (above): **super**sonic

tele- (far off): **tele**vision

trans- (across): **trans**atlantic

54

REUNION

Draw a line to show which beginnings and endings could go together and then write the whole word in the space provided. The first one has been done for you.

	Beginnings	Endings		
1.	anti	possible	1.	antidote
2.	pre	colate	2.	_____
3.	dis	phone	3.	_____
4.	im	dote	4.	_____
5.	sub	fer	5.	_____
6.	per	natural	6.	_____
7.	tele	appear	7.	_____
8.	bene	pone	8.	_____
9.	super	way	9.	_____
10.	post	volent	10.	_____

So, if I think of that little lane leading to my house, does that make me a "psychopath"?

No, Steven, it makes you a microbrain.

THE SOUND ALIKE TWINS

Don't confuse ante- and anti-. They sound alike but they are spelled differently.

If you know what they mean, you will always know which you need.

ante means before

Expectant mothers attend an *antenatal* clinic *before* their babies are born.

ante + natal = before + birth

anti means against

Motorists put *antifreeze* in their car radiators.

anti + freeze = against + freezing

Antenatal

Anti-Natal

Hello, I'm Aunty Natal.

Aunty Natal

IDENTIFY THE MISSING LETTERS

See if the prefix means before (ante) or against (anti).

ant__clockwise	in the opposite direction to the way the hands of a clock go round
ant__septic	kills microbes
ant__room	a waiting room outside a larger room
ant__dote	a medicine which stops the effects of poison
ant__cedents	ancestors
ant__diluvian	so outdated it could have happened before the Biblical flood
ant__perspirant	this stops perspiration
ant__pathy	a strong feeling of dislike
ant__podes	a place on the opposite side of the world to where you are
ant__biotic	medicine which works by killing the germs causing the illness

That's all you need to know about prefixes.

I hope that's not too much of an anti-climax.

COLIN'S CHALKBOARD CONCLUSIONS

You can add a prefix, or two,
to make a new word.

1. Learn the common prefixes.

2. Know what they mean.

Then you'll be more likely to spell the longer word accurately.

They say that pre-vention is better than cure.
That is, doing things before the problem arises
is a good idea. I suppose that . . . if I were to
mend your car before a problem arose. . .

That would be a "pre-fix".

That was my joke!

58

Just Mucking About Again

Let's talk about spoonerisms.

SPOONERISM (noun) - the swapping round of the first letters or sounds of a group of words to create a funny effect. e.g. a well-boiled icicle (a well-oiled bicycle).

That's really called METATHESIS, or changing sounds (META + THESIS).

Rev. Dr William Archibald Spooner (1844-1930) was a very clever man and warden of New College, Oxford. He didn't MEAN to muddle so many words and phrases when he spoke to his students but unfortunately he became so well known for it that such verbal muddles became named after him. In 1879 he announced the next hymn as "Kinquering Congs their titles take." Do you think the congregation sang the right words after this?

A half-formed wish.   **A half-warmed fish.**

What do you think Dr Spooner MEANT to say instead of these spoonerisms?

1. The Lord is a shoving leopard.

2. You have hissed all my mystery lectures.

3. You have tasted two whole worms.

4. Let us drink to the queer old Dean.

5. He's a boiled sprat.

Keep your ears open for spoonerisms. They usually happen in the heat of the moment. Perhaps someone will yell at you to "Doze the claw!" or "Fipe your wheat!" You probably muddled words like "carpark" when you were a child or have family spoonerisms like "chish and fips".

Once you start deliberately swapping sounds around, it gets infectious: drairhesser, prying fan, bustdin, a clicking tock . . .

Can you think of any more?

SILENT LETTERS

Did you know that over half the letters of the alphabet can be used silently in words?

Here are just three examples:

You don't hear the b in this word:

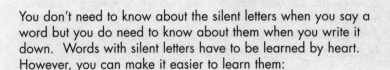

You don't hear the h in this word:

You don't hear the s in this word:

You don't need to know about the silent letters when you say a word but you do need to know about them when you write it down. Words with silent letters have to be learned by heart. However, you can make it easier to learn them:

If you think of other words in the same family where the silent letter *is* pronounced (si**g**n and si**g**nature, for example).

If you learn silent letter words in letter groups (all the silent b words together and so on).

If you can devise funny ways to remember the hard words (don't i**g**nore a **g**nu).

If you learn as much about the background of the words as you can (**sc**ience comes from Latin **sc**ire – to know).

Some letters that are silent in particular words today used to be voiced (that is, pronounced) years and years ago.

Take the word **knight**, for example. We pronounce it *nite*. Geoffrey Chaucer, who lived 600 years ago, would have pronounced the k at the beginning and would have had a go at pronouncing the gh as well. He would have said *ker-nikt*. (Say it that way to yourself when you are spelling it if it helps.)

You probably think it's strange that letters that became silent weren't dropped. You may think it even stranger that silent letters were added to some perfectly good words that didn't need them and never had needed them. The words **doute** and **dette** had a silent b added just to show that they came from the Latin words "dubitum" and "dubitare". That's how **doubt** and **debt** became such tricky words to spell.

Printers and dictionary makers did a lot of this kind of "tidying up" of the language as consistency in spelling became more and more important.

Spelling has become standardised and we now have to know where the silent letters are lurking. There are two reasons for this. If we don't our spelling will be wrong, OK? Just live with it, right? We'll look stupid, have rubbish lives, and be shunned.

Also, we do have something to thank silent letters for. Thanks to them, we know the meaning of words which would be different without them.

We know that **knit** doesn't mean **nit**.
We know that **aisle** is different from **isle**.
We know that **reign** is not the same thing as **rain** or **rein**.

And see opposite for an entirely true story about all this. Only the facts have been changed.

So, you kneed to now them. Rats. Need to know them. Let's have a look…

Spelling Mistakes
that Changed the Course of History, part 912

Here are some of the main groups.

Silent b words

The letter b, printed in bold type, is silent in the words below.

Say the words aloud without voicing the silent b but noticing that it is there.

lam**b**
bom**b**
crum**b**
dum**b**, dum**b**founded
clim**b**, clim**b**er
succum**b**

You often find silent b after m.

And remember silent b in: de**b**t dou**b**t su**b**tle

Silent c words

Look out for **sc** in words where the c is silent. Here are a few. There are lots of others. If you had only ever heard the words said and never seen them written down, you wouldn't know they each had a letter c in them.

scenery   fas**c**inate
scent   des**c**endant
dis**c**iple

I sent you some perfume –
it must have got lost in the post.
I scent a lame excuse.

DEFUSE THE SILENT BOMB

Can you unjumble these words? Like "bomb" they all end in a silent "b". And to help you concentrate, we might just have wired this book up to a silent bomb that will go off if you don't solve them all within 60 seconds starting from … NOW.

tbhmu   a digit on the hand

bmto   a burial place

mlbi   a jointed part of the body,
              such as an arm or leg

OVER TO YOU!

Can you spell these words?

_____

_____

_____

Numb hands

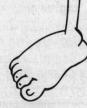

Numb feet

Numbskull

Silent g words

Say these words aloud, being careful not to voice the silent g.

gnaw   si**g**n   **g**nat   si**g**npost   **g**nash   rei**g**n
gnarled   forei**g**n   **g**nome   desi**g**n   **g**nu   campai**g**n

The combination **gn** is one to look out for, especially if you're trying to find a word in the dictionary that sounds as if it should start with n.

Sometimes other words in the same word family help, as we've said already:

si**g**n but sig-nal and sig-nature.

Some people find it helpful to *say* the g when learning to spell a silent g word:

The gnome gnawed a gnu. (The nome nawed a nu).
The ger-nome ger-nawed a ger-nu.

Silent gh words

There are lots of gh words.

some au**gh** ones:
dau**gh**ter cau**gh**t nau**gh**ty

some ei**gh** ones:
ei**gh**t   wei**gh**   nei**gh**bour   slei**gh**

i**gh** words are far more interesting:

li**gh**t   li**gh**thouse   ni**gh**t   ni**gh**tmare   si**gh**t   fi**gh**t   ri**gh**t

But the words that are the MOST interesting
are **ough** ones. See how each of these words
has a different **ough** sound!

enou**gh** (-uff)   althou**gh** (-o)   cou**gh** (-off)   bou**gh** (-ow)
throu**gh** (-oo)   bou**gh**t (-ort)

BRAIN CELL QUESTION!

Can you think of four more words spelled **-ought** that rhyme with bought?

1. _____
2. _____
3. _____
4. _____

G-WHIZZ

Match up the right definition with these silent g words.

You're allowed to use a dictionary!

a) gnocchi   1) rod on a sundial that casts the shadow

b) gnomon   2) snarl or growl

c) gnathic   3) small dumplings in a sauce

d) gnar   4) relating to the jaws

That top puzzle's difficult, isn't it. I thought I ought to do it, but however much I fought, my efforts came to nought.

It might be easier than you think, idiot.

Silent h words

Read these words. Be careful not to pronounce the h!

heir, **h**eiress, **h**eirloom
honest, **h**onesty
hour
honour
r**h**inoceros
r**h**yme
ex**h**ibit
ve**h**icle
catar**rh**
antirr**h**inum

and Jo**h**n which comes from the Latin Johannes (pronounced Jo-hann-us).

Silent k words

Steven, I'll give you £5 if you can say five words with a silent "k" before I say knife.

I won't know any. I haven't got the knack for that sort of thing. I just get my knickers knitted in a knot.

Five! Well done – but I'm afraid I've already said knife – so you're knocked out of the competition!

Silent m words

Mnemonic (pronounced NEM-ON-ICK) begins with a silent m but I'll tell you about mnemonics in the next chapter.

MISSING LETTERS

Can you complete these words?

ch – – –   several musical notes
            played together
gh – – – – – small green cucumber
            usually pickled
kh – – –   colour of army uniforms
rh – – – – – plant with thick juicy
            stems you can eat

No, I said today you should wear your *khaki* uniform.

The Importance of Spelling in Literature, part 96

**... They travelled by night
to avoid detection ...**

**... They travelled by knight
to avoid detection ...**

Silent ⓝ words

These silent n words need watching. Look at the two lists below. In the left-hand list, the n is silent in all the words. In the right-hand list, where suffixes have been added, the n is voiced.

Shhh!	*Say it!*
condemn	condem-nation
solemn	solem-nity
damn	dam-nation
autumn	autum-nal
hymn	hym-nal

Silent ⓟ words

Notice:
ras**p**berry
cu**p**board
cor**p**s
recei**p**t

and all the words we get from Greek beginning with **p**n, **p**s, **p**t.

The p is not voiced in these words.

pneumonia
pneumatic
psalm
psychology
ptarmigan
pterodactyl

What am I? Please unjumble me:

Answer: column

BRAINBOX OF THE UNIVERSE QUIZ

ps - - - - nym   (an assumed name, a pen name)
ps - - - - sis   (an itchy disease of the skin)

Pterodactyl

Terror Daryl

Silent s words

aisle   isle   island

Both isle and island come from an old English word 'iland' or 'igland'. Some clever people *added* a silent s to both words because they thought the words came from the Latin 'insula'. Now we're stuck with the results of this mistaken identity.

Did anyone notice that **ais**le has two silent letters?

Silent t words

There are two ways of saying OFTEN. How do you say it?

You can say OFF-EN (silent t).
You can say OFF-TEN (voiced t).

Both ways are correct but you must always spell the word OFTEN.

Here are some -stle words.

castle
trestle
hustle and bustle
mistletoe

And don't forget the MORTGAGE!

Here are some -sten words.

moisten
fasten
listen
christen

The Importance of Spelling in Geography, part 29

When you write about

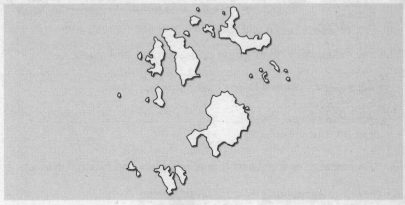

The Scilly Isles

the Scilly Isles, a group of remote and beautiful islands off the coast of Cornwall, it is important not to write about

The Silly Aisles

the Silly Aisles, which are in the National Cathedral of Gagaland, designed by Jack El-Loco in 1857.

Silent U words

I wish you were silent!

lots of words begin with **gu**.

For example, think of g**u**ide and g**u**ardian and g**u**est.

Try the test opposite to see how many you know.

And don't forget these!
bisc**u**it, b**u**oy, b**u**ilding

And remember that there is British English and North American English.

🇬🇧	🇺🇸
hono**u**r	honor
splendo**u**r	splendor
labo**u**r	labor
humo**u**r	humor
colo**u**r	color

And you always have u after q. This is easy to remember.

If there's a Q, U always joins at the back.

Silent W words

Do you know these silent w words?

wren	**w**rist
write	**w**rinkle
wrap	**w**rong

SILENT U TEST:

g**u**_____   opposite of innocent

g**u**_____   formal promise

g**u**_____   beheading machine

g**u**_____   musical instrument

We guarantee it won't actually cut your head off - or your money back!

MAGICIANS' SUPPLIES

SILENT W CROSSWORD

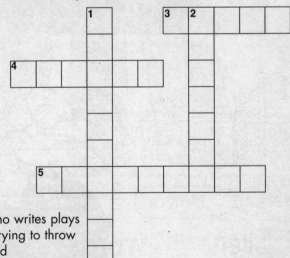

Down

1. A person who writes plays
2. To fight by trying to throw to the ground

Across

3. A weapon with a long steel blade
4. A circle of flowers and leaves
5. Destruction of a ship at sea

CoLiN'S CHALKBOARD CONCLUSIONS

SILENT LETTERS

You have to know about silent letters because:

1. Sometimes, if you leave them out, you change the meaning of the word completely.
2. Anyway, whether you think they're a good idea or not, the proper spelling of lots of words involves silent letters, and if you don't get them right you'll look stupid and generally lose marks in life.
3. So, notice them when you see them written down; invent any way you can that'll help you remember.

Silent C!

MNEMONICS

Can we have MNEMONICS now?
What ARE they?

A mnemonic is a memory trick, anything that helps you to remember dates, or spellings, or scientific facts or anything else that is important to you.

For example, as a way of remembering the points of the compass (North, East, South and West) and where they are, you can remember "**N**ever **E**at **S**oggy **W**heat", and that will remind you that the initial letters are NESW. These go clockwise around the compass like this:

The good news is that you can use mnemonics for loads of things. We'll get to the spelling ones in a moment, but let's just muck about with some others first. You may know some of these already.

COLOURS OF THE RAINBOW MNEMONIC

Richard **O**f **Y**ork **G**ave **B**attle **I**n **V**ain

R   red
O   orange
Y   yellow
G   green
B   blue
I   indigo
V   violet

RED
ORANGE
YELLOW
GREEN
BLUE
INDIGO
VIOLET

Or: **R**emember **O**nly **Y**oung **G**irls **B**elieve **I**n **V**ampires

Or: **R**ely **O**n **Y**our **G**reen **B**icycle **I**n **V**ietnam!

Or you can remember that there was an American millionaire who called himself Roy G. Biv.

It doesn't matter which sentence you remember as long as it works. Mnemonics are meant to *help* you remember. Choose whichever sentence you like best or make another one up if you prefer.

LINES ON A MUSICAL STAVE MNEMONIC

Every **G**ood **B**oy **D**eserves **F**avours

E G B D F

HISTORICAL DATE MNEMONIC

In fourteen hundred and ninety-two
Columbus sailed the ocean blue.

And discovered the West Indies.

SOPHIE
SMARTIPANTS

Thank you, Sophie. That's splendid. That's quite enough for now. We'll look at some spelling mnemonics in the next section. Ready?

SPELLING MNEMONICS

There's one very well known one which you may know too.
(Unfortunately, most people know only the first two lines).

IE/EI MNEMONIC

Put I before E
except after C
or when sounded like A
as in neighbour or weigh

Let's look at some examples to see how well the rule works.

IE	EI after C	EI sounding like A
priest, friend, field, shield, chief, thief, belief, relief, niece, piece, fierce, pierce, relieve, grieve, reprieve, achieve, shriek, siege, view, review, hygiene	ceiling, receive, receipt, deceive, perceive	neighbour, weigh, eight, weight, freight, reign, rein, vein, their, heir

That's a fantastic rule. Are there lots of exceptions?

Well, no. There really aren't many. Here are the most important ones.

1. These words are EI when you would expect them to be IE:

counter**fei**t   he**i**fer   **ei**ther   s**ei**ze   l**ei**sure
n**ei**ther   w**ei**rd   sover**ei**gn   h**ei**ght   for**ei**gn

2. Names don't follow this rule and so you have Sh**ei**la, D**ei**rdre, N**ei**l and K**ei**th.

The IE/EI rule is really useful provided that you remember the last two lines.

If you don't remember this one, you really could look **STUPID**.

Read the IE/EI mnemonic again and see how you get on with the basic MOT.

Just apply the rule.
No exceptions here.

BASIC MOT
ie or ei?

1. Conc – – t
2. Bel – – ve
3. R – – ndeer
4. Misch – – f
5. V – – l

The words in the advanced MOT are longer but the rule is just the same. One exception has been included to keep you on your toes!

ADVANCED MOT
ie or ei?

1. Ach – – vement
2. Misch – – vous
3. Handkerch – – f
4. B – – ge
5. H – – rloom
6. Gr – – vance
7. Surv – – llance
8. For – – gn
9. Interv – – w
10. Conc – – ve

Here are a few more mnemonics you may find useful.

Explanation or **explaination?**
Remember there's a **plan** in ex**plan**ation.

Here or **hear (when you mean "listen")?**
You h**ear** with your **ear**.

Friend or **freind?**

That's the **end** of my fri**end!**

Lonely or **lonley?**
One person can be l**one**ly

Lose or **loose (when you mean 'wobbly')?**
L**oo**k at my l**oo**se t**oo**th.

Necessary, neccessary, neccesary, or **necesary?**
You need **one c**ollar and **a pair of s**ocks.

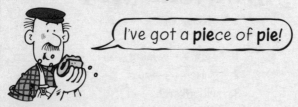

I've got a **pie**ce of **pie!**

Secertary or **secretary?**
A **secret**ary can keep a **secret**.

Separate or **seperate?**
There's **a rat** in sep **a rat** e.

Stationery or **stationary (when you mean 'not moving')?**
A station**ar**y c**ar**.

You can have fun with acrostic sentences as well. This is where each letter is used to begin a word in a sentence.

Never   **N**obody
Ever   **E**ver
Combine   **C**omes
Egg   **E**very
Sandwiches   **S**ingle
Sardines   **S**unday
And   **A**nd
Raspberry   **R**emembers
Yoghurt   **Y**ou.

Have a go yourself at making an acrostic sentence for "necessary".

N _____

E _____

C _____

E _____

S _____

S _____

A _____

R _____

Y _____

Nightly **E**xtra **C**orn **E**nsures **S**teven's **S**tumpy **A**rms **R**emain **Y**ellow.

Taking words apart

Another useful way of remembering how to spell a word is to take it apart and to be aware of how the parts fit together.

Mis + spell = mi**ss**pell (double s)
un + necessary = u**nn**ecessary (double n)
dis + appear = di**s**appear (single s)
real + ly = rea**ll**y (double l)
sincere + ly = sincer**e**ly (keep the e)

A word like **criticism** can look difficult to spell. It's much less formidable (for+mid+able) when you see that it's just critic + ism.

Word families

Use your knowledge of word families to help you with other words in the same family.

Signature will help you with **sign**.
Govern will help you with **govern**ment.
Adapt**ation** will help you with adapt**able**.
Mean will help you with **mean**t.
Gradual will help you with **gradual**ly.
Ab**sen**t will help you with ab**sen**ce.

Look carefully

Take a long hard look at words you are trying to learn. Notice anything really odd about them that may stick in your mind.

Notice the -wkw- in a**wkw**ard.
Notice the -hth- in eig**hth**.
Notice that **un**u**su**al has three **u**s.
Notice words like f**a**c**e**t**iou**s that have all five vowels in the right order.

Enjoy these oddities and spelling will be fun too.

Say the words carefully

Make sure you say words carefully. Some people misspell words because they say them wrongly.

Make sure you say:

It's the correct pro-nun-ciation you need, innit?

arctic	not artic
Antarctic	not Antarctic
burglar two syllables,	not burgular
chimney	not chimley
chocolate three syllables,	not choclate
equipment	not equiptment
expedition	not experdition
February	not Febuary
government	not goverment
gradually	not gradully
handkerchief	not hankerchief
hundred two syllables,	not hundered
information	not imformation
interesting four syllables,	not intresting
library	not libary
mischievous three syllables,	not mischievious
nephew pronounced "neffew",	not nevew
packed lunch	not pack lunch
pantomime	not pantomine
perhaps	not prehaps
probably	not propably or probally
recognise or **recognize**	not reconise or reconize
sandwich	not sanwich
secretary	not secertary
surprise	not suprise
twelfth	not twelth
umbrella	not umberella
vegetable four syllables,	not vegtable
veterinary five syllables,	not vetinary

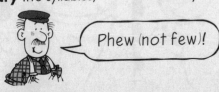

Phew (not few)!

Extra e

Do you know why you have to keep the e in the words below?

Notice + able	notic**e**able
Pronounce + able	pronounc**e**able
Service + able	servic**e**able
Change + able	chang**e**able
Venge + ance	veng**e**ance
Courage + ous	courag**e**ous

If you know about soft and hard c and g, it all makes sense and it is easier to remember.

The letter c has two sounds: either soft s or hard k.
The letter g has two sounds: either soft j or hard g.
The letters c and g are usually hard in front of a, o, u: cat, cot, cut; gap, got, gun.

They are usually soft in front of e, i, y: cell, cider, cycle; germ, ginger, gym.

By keeping the e in words like notic**e**able and courag**e**ous, you keep the c and g soft.

88

Soft and hard c
WORDSEARCH

Find these words in the wordsearch square:

cavity	compass	cider	coin
century	cast	coast	circle
certain	cycle		

Words may be arranged vertically, horizontally or diagonally and may be written forwards or backwards. The same letter can be used more than once.

```
C  O  A  S  T  Z  R  A

E  A  D  J  V  E  B  C

N  L  V  C  D  U  E  O

T  R  C  I  N  R  L  M

U  P  C  R  T  M  C  P

R  O  G  A  I  Y  Y  A

Y  S  I  H  S  C  C  S

T  N  I  O  C  T  R  S
```

How many "soft c" words did you find?
How many "hard c" words did you find?

Without looking at the list of words that you need to say carefully (on page 87) see if you can complete these words from memory.

WHICH LETTERS ARE MISSING?

1. sec – – tary
2. vet – – inary
3. han – kerchief
4. Feb – uary
5. pro – ably

Extra k

picnic + ing = picnicking

Now that you know about soft and hard c, can you work out
why we have to add a k to "picnicking"?

The answer is that without the k, "cing" would sound like "sing"
as it does in the word "icing".

Do these word sums, putting in the extra k where it is needed.

Remember that c is soft
(sounds like s)
in front of e, i, y.

TEST YOUR SKILL

1. panic + s   _____
2. panic + y   _____
3. mimic + ing   _____
4. mimic + ed   _____
5. mimic + ry   _____
6. picnic + er   _____
7. picnic + ed   _____
8. picnic + s   _____

Steven has NOT read this section very carefully.

Will you mark his spelling test for him and tell him his score?

(Would you be kind enough to write his corrections for him beside any words he has got wrong?)

Steven S. Monster

1 Receive
2 Separate
3 Sincerley
4 Freind
5 Lonley
6 Panicks
7 Intrested
8 Realy
9 Necessary
10 Couragous

Score: **/10**

Comment:

Marker's initials:

Well, if you're so clever, can you spell these words:

Steven, don't you think it's a bit easy given that you've written them out?

Pronounceable
Handkerchief
Signature
Unnecessary
Expedition

COLIN'S CHALKBOARD CONCLUSIONS

1. Put i before e except after c, or when sounded like a, as in neighbour and weigh. (Only a few exceptions).
2. Think of your own silly sentences for tricky words (like, "a secretary can keep a secret").
3. Take words apart (separating prefixes and suffixes to see how the word is made up).
4. If you need a soft c or g, you'll probably need an -e to follow them.
5. Add k to c to make it hard.

Use as many mnemonics as you like to remember those tricky spellings. Do you know about Mnemonics?

Can't remember him.

PREFIX

USEFUL LISTS
TRICKY WORDs

Most people will find these words difficult to spell. Remember they are here when you want to use them. Best of all, learn them by heart as soon as you can.

absolutely
across
address
afraid
among
amount
annoy
any
apology
argument
autumn

beautiful
because
before
broken
burglar
business

character
chocolate
college
completely

definitely
describe
description
different
difficult

embarrass
especially
excellent
except
excitement
exercise
exhausted
explanation
extraordinary

family

fascinating
favourite
finish
fortunately
frightened

gradually
grateful
guess

heard
honestly
horrible
humorous

immediately
information
innocent
intelligent
interesting
invisible

jealous

library
luxury

mention
mischievous
moment

necessary
neighbour

obedient
occasionally
opinion
opportunity

paid
parent
passenger
perhaps

pleasant
possible
possibly
probably

realise (-ize)
really
recent
recognise (-ize)
referee
responsible
ridiculous

sandwich
scissors
separate
separately
severely
similar
sincerely
soldier
sometimes
speech
suggest
suppose
surely
surprise

tired
tomorrow

until
useful
usually

valuable
vegetable
vehicle

woman
women
woollen

NUMBERS

When you write stories, poems, plays and letters, you will generally write numbers in words instead of figures - and some are quite tricky to spell. There is no rule for these, you just have to learn them. Take particular care with these numbers:

twelve	second
fourteen	fifth
fifteen	eighth
nineteen	ninth
forty	twelfth
ninety-nine	fifteenth
one hundred	twentieth

The only numbers that need hyphens are combination numbers up to 99.

So. You've read the book. You've done the tests. Are you a spelling genius?

Well, if you're normal, probably not quite yet. But we've got four tips to help you on your way:

Make yourself a spelling notebook.
Writing any words you seem to use a lot in a handy book can save you time when you're looking them up and help you learn them.

Find a good dictionary.
Make sure you use a dictionary which is well laid out and easy to understand - they're not all the same!

Always check your work.
Read through everything you write to make sure you haven't made any careless mistakes. Check the spelling of any words that you're not sure of.

And . . . take pride in what you do.
Make everything that you write as good as you can. Spelling is a bit like life; most of it's down to you. So good luck, and may the spelling force be with you!

95

ANSWERS
(page numbers are in brackets)

MORE THAN ONE
Basic MOT (19) 1. books,
2. wishes, 3. teachers, 4. pens,
5. glasses.
Advanced MOT (19)
1. winches, 2. ruminants,
3. blemishes, 4. mnemonics
5. zygoranismagicianisticalists.
Basic MOT (22) 1. flies,
2. toys, 3. bullies, 4. holidays,
5. donkeys, 6. berries, 7. spies,
8. stories, 9. valleys, 10. ponies.
Advanced MOT (23)
1. essays, 2. fantasies,
3. opportunities, 4. factories,
5. volleys, 6. universities,
7. qualities, 8. pulleys,
9. responsibilities, 10. convoys.
Odd One Out (25) shelf (shelves)
Find the Mystery Word (26)
The mystery word is *sheaves* 1.
ladies, 2. witches, 3. women,
4. potatoes, 5. knives,
6. children, 7. sopranos.

ADDING ENDINGS
Vital Missing Letter (30)
1. y, 2. i, 3. y, 4. i, 5. i.
Advanced MOT (31) 1. i,
2. i, 3. y, 4. i, 5. y, 6. i, 7. y,
8. i, 9. i, 10. i.
Sophie's Test (32) 1. ✓,
2. careless, 3. ✓, 4.sincerely,
5.safety.
Henry VIII's letter (33)
writing, lonely, definitely,
hoping, grateful, sincerely.

HOMOPHONES
Missing partners (38)
whole, tale, thrown, would,
son, *son*, thrown, for, *whole*,
tale, *would*, profit, isle, meddle,
hymn, sealing.
Missing pairs (39) male/mail
die/dye, heel/heal, alter/altar.
Zandra's letter (40)
1. deer/dear, 2. wood/would,
3. yew/you, 4. hole/whole,
5. weak/week, 6.beech/beach,
7. grate/great, 8. right/write
9. yew/you,10. reed/read.
Missing letters (40) hoarse,
some, meat, allowed, cheque.
Testing, Testing (41)
1. who's, 2. hear, 3. too/to/two
4. it's, 5. know/no.
Test Your Understanding
(43) bought, where, were,

clothes, off.
Homographs (45)
ENtrance way in,
enTRANCE bewitch, delight,
PERmit written permission,
perMIT allow,
CONduct behaviour,
conDUCT lead,
EXtract small part from whole,
exTRACT draw out,
REfuse rubbish,
reFUSE say no.

ADDING BEGINNINGS
Whole word prefixes (49)
OUT
outcast, outburst, outlaw,
outskirts.
OVER
overcharge, overbalance,
overflow, overboard.
UNDER
underwear, underline,
undergrowth, underhand
UP
upset, upright, uproar, upheaval.
Test Your Word Power (51)
1. disobey, 2. incorrect,
3. unnecessary, 4. misbehave,
5. illegal, 6. impatient
The mystery word is *double*.
Find the words (53)
centipede, trident, decathlon.
Reunion (55) 2. prefer,
3. disappear, 4. impossible,
5. subway, 6. percolate,
7. telephone, 8. benevolent,
9. supernatural, 10. postpone.
Identify the missing letters
(57) anticlockwise, antiseptic,
anteroom, antidote,
antecedents, antediluvian,
antiperspirant, antipathy,
antipodes, antibiotic.
Spoonerisms (60) 1. The
Lord is a loving shepherd.
2. You have missed all my
history lectures.
3. You have wasted two whole
terms. 3. Let us drink to the
dear old Queen. 4. He's a
spoiled brat.

SILENT LETTERS
Defuse the Silent Bomb
(65) thumb, tomb, limb.
Over to You (65) scissors,
scythe, muscle.

Brain cell question (67)
(more answers possible) sought,
fought, brought, wrought.
G-Whizz
(67) a=3, b=1, c=4, d=2.
Missing Letters (69)
chord, gherkin, khaki, rhubarb.
Brainbox of the Universe
(71) pseudonym, psoriasis,
Silent U Test (75) guilty,
guarantee, guillotine, guitar.
Silent W Crossword (75)
Down 1. playwright,
2. wrestle.
Across 3. sword, 4. wreath,
5. shipwreck.

MNEMONICS
Basic MOT (83) 1. conceit,
2. believe, 3. reindeer,
4. mischief, 5. veil.
Advanced MOT (83)
1. achievement, 2. mischievous,
3. handkerchief, 4. beige,
5. heirloom, 6. grievance,
7. surveillance, 8. foreign,
9. interview, 10. conceive.
Wordsearch (89)
5 soft c words, 5 hard c words.

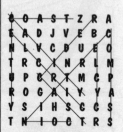

Which letters are missing
(89) 1. secretary, 2. veterinary,
3. handkerchief, 4. February,
5. probably.
Test your skills (90)
1. panics, 2. panicky,
3. mimicking, 4. mimicked,
5. mimicry, 6. picnicker,
7. picnicked, 8. picnics.
Steven's Spelling Test (91)
1. ✓, 2. ✓, 3. sincerely,
4. friend, 5. lonely, 6. panics,
7. interested, 8. really, 9. ✓,
10. courageous.
Score: 3/10

PUNCTUATION REPAIR KIT

Why bother?

Punctuation matters.
For exams, life, everything.
You need to say what you mean.
You should mean what you say.
You don't want to look stupid!

PUNCTUATION
REPAIR KIT

WILLIAM VANDYCK

Illustrated by David Farris

Hodder
Children's
Books

a division of Hodder Headline Limited

This book is dedicated to my friend,
Snidey Kathy.

W.V.

CONTENTS

CONTENTS

INTRODUCTION

The Big Question: Why Bother?

Punctuation matters. Just accept it.
A lot of people say…

But what about all those really difficult hurdles in life?

Like schoolwork?

Exams?

Getting interviews for jobs?

Getting on in your job?

Hmm? What are they all saying?

Well, put it this way: you can go a long way in all things in life if you observe

GOLDEN RULE NUMBER ONE

It is simple.
It is easy to remember.
It is **absolutely crucial.**
And it is over the page.

DON'T LOOK STUPID!

There are right ways to punctuate, and there are wrong ways.

If you use the wrong way, it might not be clear what you're saying. Or, worse, you may be saying something you don't mean. What will people think?

Hmm. That's strange! She must have known that this was an important piece of writing in its own way. Yet she hasn't bothered —or perhaps doesn't know how— to punctuate properly.

OLD BAT

FRIEND BOYFRIEND TEACHER EXAMINER EMPLOYER

I can't read this without my glasses.

ALERT! ALERT! RUBBISH LIFE AHEAD!

Now, this book is going to help. And you won't be alone in your learning.

We're going to go to the Repair Kit Garage. I'd like you to meet the mechanics.

Here's Zelda. Say hello, Zelda.

Hello. Welcome to the garage.

Here's Steven, the Stupid Monster. Say hello, Steven.

Goodbye... Oh – what was the question again?

Oh dear. Here's Colin.

Hello, I want to be a teacher. I may sound dull, but I do collect milk bottle tops. I know that sounds a bit dull too. It is, I suppose. In fact, it's pretty much a waste of time. Sorry!

Er, thank you, Colin. Well, you have a quick practice at being a teacher. Steven can make some tea, and we'll make a start.

9

SENTENCES AND PARAGRAPHS

POW!

First, we'll look at possibly the hardest thing to lay down fixed rules about in the whole of the English language! How about that? We are clearly not messing about here. Oh no, we are cracking on with the difficult issues straight away.

Whhyyy start with something hard?

It's like understanding about car engines. A car engine is easy to recognise, but it's a bit difficult to say exactly what a car engine *is* because there are so many different types. Once you understand what a car engine is, you'll find it easier to understand the individual bits inside it.

It's the same with sentences and paragraphs. Like car engines, they are easy to spot, and hard to define. But it will help you to understand and use bits of punctuation if you first get a general idea of what sentences and paragraphs are all about.

So, here's what you need to know about sentences and paragraphs.

SENTENCES
The Easy Bit

First, a rule which is very easy and tremendously important.

Every sentence starts with a capital letter and finishes with a full stop.
Like that one – and this one.

Hi, I'm Raoul the Rule-Avoider. Any exceptions here? I'm here to tell you if rules can be broken.

There are no exceptions, OK? None! Not even question marks (?) and exclamation marks (!) like the ones I've just used. We'll be dealing with those later, but for the moment, just remember that they have built-in full stops at the bottom. So they do end sentences by making sure the full stop is there! Understand?

It is a fantastically easy rule to remember. Because it is fantastically easy, if you get it wrong, you will absolutely, definitely, no-doubt-about-it, look

STUPID.

Enjoy this moment. Savour it for all you can. This rule about sentences is one of the few things in punctuation that has no exceptions. Take any page of this book. Or any book. You should find that every single sentence begins with a capital letter and ends with a full stop. This is so straightforward that even Steven should be able to get it right.

Oh, and thanks for the tea, Steven.

i sentence myself to death for forgetting to put a capital letter at the beginning of this sentence.

This is known as capital punishment.

OK. We've dealt with the bits at the ends of sentences. But what goes in the middle? This is not so easy.

Probably the best way to think about a sentence is to remember two things:

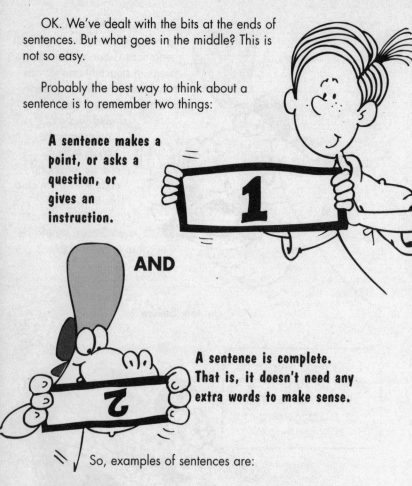

A sentence makes a point, or asks a question, or gives an instruction.

AND

A sentence is complete. That is, it doesn't need any extra words to make sense.

So, examples of sentences are:

The rain fell.
That sentence about the rain was really boring.
The man's head came clean off.
That's better, isn't it?
Don't answer back.

Have a quick check that those sentences stick to our two rules.

Remember that you can't tell a sentence by how long it is.

In fact, by making one of our example sentences longer, we can actually stop it being a sentence. For example:

The rain fell. **←———— This is a sentence.**
Although the rain fell. **←———— This is not a sentence.**

The last example isn't really complete, is it? The word "Although" suggests that something happened **despite** the rain. Yet we don't know what it is. We're left hanging in the air.

Was the rain hanging in the air?

No, but you will be if you interrupt like that.

But we can make it back into a sentence again by completing the sense. For example, by saying:

Although the rain fell, the game continued.

Now there is a complete point. That's what we can call a sentence.

Try these examples. Which of them do you think are sentences?

Question 1
a) Spinning wildly through the air, humming quietly.
b) She bit him.

Answer 1
a) No. Obviously there's lots going on (and it all sounds very exciting). But it's not complete in sense, is it? We need some extra words for the sense to be complete.
b) Yes! It may be short but it makes a point and it is complete. You don't need extra words for it to make sense on its own. It sounds quite fun.

Now have a go at making sentences from the following passage.

Question 2
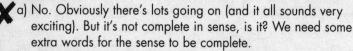
there was a terrible collision on the motorway a lorryload of jelly wobbled so much that it fell into the road this caused a lorry carrying custard to slide into a van delivering sponge cake local residents sprinkled hundreds and thousands onto the resulting mixture to stop it being so slippery the police said that traffic would be a trifle delayed

In case you thought punctuation was pointless, look how much easier this is to read when it's properly punctuated.

Answer 2
There was a terrible collision on the motorway. A lorryload of jelly wobbled so much that it fell into the road. This caused a lorry carrying custard to slide into a van delivering sponge cake. Local residents sprinkled hundreds and thousands onto the resulting mixture to stop it being so slippery. The police said that traffic would be a trifle delayed.

Hold onto your hats because here's where we enter "Sometimes it's OK to break the rules" territory. Look at this passage.

Ah ha! About time we had an exception!

Zelda threw herself out of the way of the car. A squeal of brakes. The crunch of metal. Glass smashing. Flames. An explosion. And then, more frightening still, silence.

Obviously the writer of this piece of action fiction hasn't used full sentences, but the short sentences are used to speed up the pace of the writing. It would have been a bit dull if it had read:

There was a squeal of brakes. Then there was a sound of metal crunching. Then there was the sound of glass smashing...

Style is one of the main reasons it's sometimes difficult to say exactly what a sentence is and isn't. But don't let that get you down. If you remember the general rules, you'll have a much better idea of when you can break them, and when other people who are breaking them are being stylish... or

STUPID.

Problems

Often people use full stops where there doesn't appear to be a full sentence. Sometimes they are being stupid, eg. Although it was raining. But sometimes it's OK just to use a bit of a sentence.

GREETINGS

You'll probably find it easier to think of these as exceptions. In fact, often they're short versions of sentences which were so frequently used that people didn't bother getting to the end of them. ("Morning" is short for "Good morning", which is short for "I wish you a good morning", and "Wotcha" is short for "What have you been getting up to, then?".)

QUESTIONS AND ORDERS

We've already said that a sentence can give instructions and ask questions, but we also said that a sentence should be complete in itself. You might think that "Don't!" and "Why not?" aren't complete. But because these words are usually only said in response to something happening, or in answer to something someone says, they usually do make sense on their own. For instance, if you were about to strike a match and someone said "Don't!", to which you replied, "Why not?" these words would make sense. They would be short for:

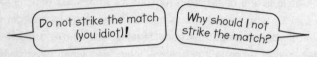

ANSWERS

"A bucketful of spanners" is not a sentence because it doesn't make sense on its own. But if it were the answer to a question it would make sense, be complete and be followed by a full stop. So answers which aren't really sentences can end in full stops.

PARAGRAPHS
The Easy Bit

A paragraph contains a sentence or a number of sentences. It always starts on a new line. It is usually indented (which means the first line begins slightly in from the left-hand side of the page.)

The Useful Bit

How long should sentences and paragraphs be? When do you need to start a new sentence or a whole new paragraph?

The best general rule is:

Think of your reader. Think what would make things easier to read and understand.

Really, it's a matter of style and judgment. A good general tip is to keep your writing lively by having sentences of different lengths.

Someone once said that a paragraph is "A unit of thought, not of length... " This is a pretty good way of thinking about it. A paragraph ends where you've come to a break in a thought, or a topic, or a section of description. In this break the reader and the writer can draw breath. The next thing will be something new – which is why it is started on a new line.

Next time you write, try it out!

The bad news is that you can't just start a new paragraph every time you start a new sentence. And you can't ignore paragraphs either. See if you can find a page in a book with no paragraphs. Doesn't it look terrible? Is that how you want your writing to look?

The good news is that as long as you stick to the general rules, you'll do just fine.

Let's try another way of looking at it. What's the one thing on a car that you really must have?

Fluffy dice? Car sweets? Go faster stripes?

Brakes?

DON'T KNOW ABOUT PUNCTUATION

Thank you, Zelda. You need brakes because you can't just go on and on. Sometimes you just have to stop. It's the same when you're writing – it's important to make sure the breaks work. This is why you use sentences and paragraphs.

Three helpful hints

1 Short sentences are easier to understand, but don't use only short ones. You can. If you want to. But it's jerky. It's a bit irritating. Isn't it?

2 Long sentences are sometimes more elegant than a series of short ones but if you make them too long, or have too many long ones, your reader may get a bit lost, or bored; I mean by the time a sentence has been going on as long as this one, you've really got to wonder whether it wouldn't be better to have several sentences instead, haven't you? Hello? Is there anyone still reading this bit?

3 You will get a better feel for paragraphing if you take a look at what other people do. Next time you're reading something, keep an eye on when the writer has started a new paragraph, and ask yourself, "Why?".

I do want to make this absolutely clear—I know it's a bit boring, but you have to be sensible.

COLIN'S CONCLUSIONS PAGE

A sentence:
always starts with a capital letter
always ends with a full stop
makes sense on its own and usually makes a point, asks a question or gives an instruction.

A paragraph:
always starts on a new line
is usually indented
provides a break to show the reader that one section is over and a new one is beginning.

CAPITAL LETTERS

The purpose of capital letters is to make something easier to read and understand. They do this in a number of ways. Using capital letters is not a matter of personal choice or style. You have to get it right or look **STUPID.**

When to use a capital letter

THE PERSONAL PRONOUN "I"

You use a capital letter when you say "I" for example,

I hope I never have to repeat this.

Fact box

Turkish is the only language in the whole world in which the capital "I" is dotted. So, don't dot your capital "I", unless you're writing Turkish.

BEGINNING EVERY SENTENCE

We have already looked at this. If you've forgotten, slap yourself in the face with a wet fish, then go back to the beginning of the book.

BEGINNING A QUOTATION OF SOMEONE'S SPEECH

For example:

The man sat up and said, "Call that a punch?"

PEOPLE'S NAMES

Names are easy:

James, Kathy, Postman Pat —
these all have capital letters.

Some people say I'm a dimwit,
Some people say I'm thick,
But all of them have to admit,
That I can write poems that rhyme,
well, apart from this one.

BEGINNING OF EACH LINE IN POETRY

PROPER NOUNS

Well, this is tricky, but understanding the difference between a proper noun and other words helps to avoid the most common mistakes with capital letters.

First you should know that when a word names – "identifies" – a thing, we call it a noun. So, nouns include: dog, pavement, time, panic. (From the last two examples, you'll see that it's not always objects – it can be things you can't hold or look at).

Now, when a noun is being used as a name, or part of a name for a specific person or thing, it is called a "proper noun" and gets a capital letter.

Zelda, could you give us an example?

Jargon Alert! Jargon Alert! What is a proper noun?

JARGON MONSTER

The only prince I have met is Prince Charles, whose dog I fed.

The straightforward naming word is "prince". There are many princes but there is one particular prince that Zelda is talking about here – Prince Charles.

So, the very same word (prince) gets used with and without a capital letter – what matters is not the word itself but **how** the word is being used.

ROYAL DOGGY CHOCS

23

The following are sometimes listed as the types of names which need capital letters

- Books, songs, plays, etc.: "Charlie and the Chocolate Factory"

- People: Mrs Evans, Sir Lancelot, Lady Penelope, Little Lord Fauntleroy

- Organisations, events, etc.: The Post Office (but "the post office at the corner")

Are there any other times when we should use capital letters?

- Countries, towns, rivers, etc.: Patagonia, London, Finsbury Park, the Mississippi River

- Planets: Saturn, Pluto

Please, no more!

- Nicknames: "Dopey" Kent, "Kippers" Hancock

- Deity: God, Buddha, Allah. Carry this on if you're talking about Him, His, He, etc.: God spoke, and He was angry.

- Days, months, etc.: Monday, January, Christmas Day

- Rulers/titles: Duke of York, The Queen of England (but "a meal fit for a queen")

- Geographical areas: The West (as opposed to the direction – to the west)

- Brand names: You can clean your room with a hoover or a Hoover, really. Strictly speaking it should have a capital letter, but the word has become so commonly used for "vacuum cleaner" that it is OK to use it without one. The same goes for "biro" but not Ray-bans, yet, dudes.

Try putting in the capital letters.

Question 1

the goalkeeper, peter bonnetti, was known as "the cat" because he was as agile as a cat.

[start of sentence]

[We are just talking about one goalkeeper, but it's just a noun – not a proper noun – as the word goalkeeper isn't being used as part of the name of the goalkeeper.]

Answer 1

The goalkeeper, Peter Bonetti, [name] was known as "The Cat" [name] because he was as agile as a cat.

[No capital letter as it is just a noun, not part of a name.]

Question 2

although he always wanted to travel north to the north pole, there were few banks in the west who would pay him these days. still he said he had to start by the first of january so i wished him the best of luck and told him not to worry that his nickname was "the absolute loser".

[name]

[start of sentence]   [name of area, rather than direction]

Answer 2

Although he always wanted to travel north to the North Pole, there were few banks in the West who would pay him these days. Still he said he had to start by the first of January, so I wished him the best of luck and told him not to worry that his nickname was, "The Absolute Loser".

[easy]   [nickname]   [name of month]

25

FULL STOPS

There are two uses for full stops. One is to show the end of a sentence, as we have already seen. The other is for abbreviations.

Jargon Alert!
Jargon Alert!
What are abbreviations?

Abbreviations are just shortened versions of words, and sometimes you use a full stop in them. For example, "U.S.A." is an abbreviation of "United States of America".

There are two rules that you should know about abbreviations.

1 When you're putting initials in place of first names, you always put a full stop after each initial. For example, William George Vandyck can be written W.G.Vandyck.

The second rule is that when a word is contracted so that you're left with an abbreviation made up of the first and last letters of the word, you don't have to put a full stop. So:

2 Mr (Mister) Thompson killed Dr (Doctor) Evans on Mt (Mount) Everest with Lt (Lieutenant) Smith's hockey stick.

OK, now you know what it's all about, put your hand over the right-hand side of the next page and see if you know abbreviations for those on the left-hand side.

December	Dec.
Mister	Mr
Her Majesty's Ship Dreadnought	H.M.S. Dreadnought
Automobile Association	A.A.
Royal Automobile Club	R.A.C.
British Broadcasting Corporation	B.B.C. or BBC
European Union	E.U. or EU
leg before wicket	l.b.w. or lbw
eight o'clock in the morning	8:00 a.m. or 8.00 am
For example	e.g. or eg

Hold on, hold on!
What on earth is going on here?
B.B.C. or BBC?
Don't you know the answers?

Yes, I know, I'm sorry, but the fact is that apart from the two rules I mentioned, it's a bit vague. There isn't much of a general rule. What keeps happening is that a perfectly reasonable abbreviation gets made up, like "B.B.C.", then it gets used so often that the full stops get dropped. Nowadays people tend to write BBC, rather than B.B.C. On the others, the full stops are being dropped more and more, but you still can't really say that putting them in is wrong.

If you're in doubt, put them in.

QUESTION MARKS AND EXCLAMATION MARKS

Question Marks
A Question Mark Looks Like This: ?

The rule is quite simple. If someone is asking a direct question, put a question mark at the end of it.

Now, although the rule has no exceptions, there is one thing that sometimes causes confusion.

> What do you call a man with a plank on his head?
> Edward.

DIRECT AND INDIRECT QUESTIONS

It is important to tell the difference between "direct" questions and "indirect" questions.

Jargon Alert! Jargon Alert! What are these direct and indirect questions?

It's best explained by examples.

Look at this conversation:

"Can you keep quiet?" I asked him.

"Do you want a punch in the mouth?" he replied.

Now, these are called **direct** questions. The direct question is the question exactly as it was spoken – with a question mark at the end of it.

Instead, of course, you could decide to write about the same conversation like this:

I asked him if he could keep quiet. He asked me whether I wanted a punch in the mouth.

These are called **indirect** questions. "Indirect" means that we don't actually hear the question itself but instead we are told indirectly what the question was.

Any question in the whole world can be set out directly or indirectly, and you only put a question mark if it's direct.

Okay, your turn. Where should you have question marks in this lot?

Terry was thinking about what he should do.
"Do you want to go out" June asked, hopefully.
"With you" he asked. She looked me at him angrily and wondered if he thought she could mean anyone else. "Do you really think I want to go out with you" he laughed, heading for the balcony. She picked up the huge teddy bear with "Will you marry me" on its T shirt - was it really only two weeks ago that he had given it to her - and flung it at him.

Here are the answers. [Yes! Direct question]

[No question mark – indirect question.]

Terry was thinking about what he should do. "Do you want to go out?" June asked, hopefully.

[No. Indirect question.]

[Yes! Direct question]

"With you?" he asked. She looked at him angrily and wondered if he thought she could mean anyone else. "Do you really think I want to go out with you?" he laughed, heading for the balcony. She picked up the huge teddy bear with "Will you marry me?" on its T shirt - was it really only two weeks ago that he had given it to her? - and flung it at him.

[Yes! Direct question]

[Yes! Direct question - it's the T shirt that's asking the question!]

[Yes - a sneaky direct question in her thoughts]

Have you finished? Let's move on to the exclamation mark...

[Yes! Direct question]

31

Exclamation Marks

An Exclamation Mark Looks Like This: !

You shouldn't use it too often and there are three things to remember about it.

You can use it for emphasis. You can use it to show humour. You can use it for irony.

First let's look at **emphasis.**

From the name "exclamation mark" you can tell that it means that something is being "exclaimed". So shout it out! Give it more emphasis – like this!

Now how about **humour?**

Sometimes people add an exclamation mark to a sentence to make it clear that they mean it to be funny. It's like adding a wink at the end. For example:

Jason fell over – it served him right!

For this term's play, we would be grateful if parents could send in any old sheets – washed whiter than white first, please!

If there were no exclamation marks after these, they would still make perfect sense, but they would seem to be much more serious wouldn't they?

Irony is less obvious, but don't panic! You'll probably get the hang of it quite quickly. This is a bit like the "humour" point. Sometimes people get across what they mean by saying the opposite in a particular tone of voice. This is called "irony", or, if it's insulting, "sarcasm".

Jargon Alert! Jargon Alert! What is this irony?

For example, imagine Zelda lent Steven her tools and that he broke them, and didn't offer to replace them. Zelda might say:

> I think that this is not very friendly. I feel unable to rely on you further. You get no thanks from me for this behaviour.

But come on, get real! No one talks like this. She's much more likely to say the following, in a slightly sarcastic tone of voice which makes it clear that she means the opposite:

> Well, you're a really good friend. I really feel I can rely on you. Thanks a lot.

Now we have a small problem. If you just write the words out, they obviously mean the opposite of what Zelda says. So, what we do is add an exclamation mark to show that Zelda's words are meant to be ironic:

> Well, you're a really good friend! I really feel I can rely on you. Thanks a lot!

Don't Overuse It!

It's as simple as that! It's easy to see why you shouldn't! It becomes extremely hard to read! Really trying! Remember – some people don't like to read them at all! Let alone several on the same page! So before you use two or more together like this !!, or this !!!, just remember this: Don't look

STUPID.

COMMAS

A Comma Looks Like This:,

It is tremendously useful because it does all sorts of jobs. Often people use it in the wrong way which makes them look **stupid** in all sorts of ways. So settle down, because this one is going to take the longest to go through.

Different Pauses

As you know, a full stop brings a sentence to an end. Well, basically, a comma means a slight pause in a sentence.

We'll come to the many uses of these pauses in a moment, but first, this:

All commas are pauses, but not all pauses are commas.

Sometimes the pause is dealt with best by finishing the sentence, and starting a new one.

Sometimes you show a pause in a sentence in a different way; by a semi-colon perhaps – or a dash (or brackets) – or a colon:

Sometimes where you would pause if you were reading aloud, you don't need to put anything. For example, imagine you are telling someone this news-story joke:

> Every half an hour, a person is knocked down in a road traffic accident. He's sick and tired of it.

When telling this you might very well pause slightly after "every half an hour". But the words "Every half an hour a person is knocked down… " make sense (and in the way you want them to) without a pause, so you don't need the comma.

OK. Now let's have a look at the different uses of the comma.

But I've got the general idea that a comma means a slight pause in a sentence —whhyyy do I need to know any more than that?

As you'll see, you can make yourself look very **stupid** if you don't use commas correctly. Whether you should use one, and where you should put it if you do, depends on what you are trying to say. This is why we need to consider all these various uses separately. Just for now, Why Baby, bear in mind this true story about someone who didn't use a comma correctly.

In the U.S.A. the government wanted to allow fruit-plants to be duty free. So no-one would have to pay a tax if they wanted to bring them into the country. But instead of writing:

All foreign fruit-plants are free from duty.

a clerk wrote:

All foreign fruit, plants are free from duty.

That meant that there were two things that were duty free: all fruit and all plants. So the government wouldn't get tax on all sorts of things – not just fruit-plants.

A tiny slip cost the government millions of dollars and made them look

STUPID.

Uses of a Comma

We've seen that commas are usually used as a way of separating the words within a sentence to make it easier to understand. Here is a list of ways commas can do this. We'll come back and consider each of them separately:

To set apart extra points
Colin was, despite his dull stories, the most exciting tiddlywink player of his generation.

To separate items in a list
Please place all watches, rings, jewellery, silly hats, money and valuables in the hotel safe.

To set apart the people being addressed from the rest of the sentence
It seemed like a good idea at the time, officer.

To introduce direct speech
The man ran across the beach shouting, "Jellyfish! Jellyfish!"

To introduce questions
You are going to give me this video back, aren't you?

To emphasise something
I started fighting because I felt like it, that's why.

To balance two things that are being compared
The taller they are, the farther they have to reach for their shoelaces.

Right, let's go through them.

Colin was, despite his dull stories, the most exciting tiddlywink player of his generation.

You can use commas to show which words are the main part of a sentence and which are less important, extra points.

In our example, the main point is that Colin was the most exciting tiddlywink player. There is an extra point, which is that this was even though he told really boring stories. We put the commas around the extra point to make it clear for the reader.

When we use them like this, commas are like brackets (which we haven't looked at yet, but which look like this). But there is a difference between commas and brackets. You always have to use two brackets, but you can use just one comma together with the break that you get with the start and finish of the sentence. For example, the news about Colin could be written like this:

Despite his dull stories, Colin was the most exciting tiddlywink player of his generation.

or

Colin was the most exciting tiddlywink player of his generation, despite his dull stories.

In all three examples the words "despite his dull stories" are clearly packaged off. In our first example, they're packaged off between the two commas. In the last, it's between the comma and the end of the sentence.

If I can do this with brackets, whhyyy do I need to think about it with commas?

A fair question. Here are the reasons.

Style

It's good to be able to do the same thing in a number of different ways – this will stop your writing from becoming boring. The sentence looks smoother without big brackets cluttering it up.

Sense

This is really, really important. If you know how to section off words with commas, you will avoid some of the most **stupid** things that people do with punctuation.

Curse of the Killer Commas

They're out, of control.
And nothing, will ever, be quite, clear, again.
Appearing, now all over writing, everywhere.

Sometimes you must separate a word or a group of words from the rest of the sentence. Other times, you **must not.** Clearly, you need to know which one you're dealing with.

Look at this first example:

When I broke my leg a doctor was, happily, passing by.

This is fine. The main point of the sentence is that a doctor just happened to be walking past when I broke my leg. The word "happily" is an extra comment – telling us that the doctor passing by was a good thing. Because it's an extra comment, it's packaged off with the commas. So far, so good.

Now, just think how different the sense is if the commas are not there.

When I broke my leg a doctor was happily passing by.

Because the word "happily" hasn't been packaged off, it seems to be part of the main action. It makes it sound as if the doctor was passing by in a happy way. Of course, that might have been what happened, but if it's not what you meant to say, don't say it.

When I broke my leg a doctor was, happily, passing by.

When I broke my leg a doctor was happily passing by.

I'll just, separate, everything, off, then.

No, Steven! Sometimes separating the words out makes you look very **stupid** indeed. Here's the rule:

When the words are needed for the sentence to make sense, and are **not** just an extra point, they should not be separated from the rest of the sentence.

Are the following right or wrong?

Questions

a) Ping-pong balls, made of steel, are not used in ping-pong tournaments.

b) Fish, living in water, are unaffected by air pollution.

c) Chinese men, who are over six feet six inches tall, are few and far between.

Answers

a) Wrong! By putting the words "made of steel" in between commas, they are made to look like extra information not needed for the sense. In other words, it looks as if the main part of the sentence is that ping-pong balls are not used in ping-pong tournaments, and by the way they are made of steel.

b) Correct! All fish live in water, so you don't need the words "living in water". They are only there for emphasis, and so they can be packaged off with commas.

c) Wrong! I hope you got this one. Again, by packaging off the words with the commas, it looks as if we have two pieces of information. One is that Chinese men are few and far between, and the other is that Chinese men are over six and a half feet tall. Drop the commas and you'll see it makes sense.

SEPARATING ITEMS IN A LIST

Please place all watches, rings, jewellery, silly hats, money and valuables in the hotel safe.

If you want to write a list of things, the comma makes it easy to show which words are items on the list, and where the sense of the sentence starts again.

For safety reasons please do not take toys, rubber rings, submarines and pets into the pool.

Brenda Fishface
Lifeguard

You can see how helpful and important this is if you're listing groups of words, not just single words. Exactly the same rule applies:

For safety reasons please do not take silly toys, rubber rings of any description, submarines over 10 metres in length and dirty pets into the pool.

Doug E. Paddle

Imagine that without the commas. Nightmare.

It doesn't, of course, have to be a list of objects. You can have a list of events:

She came home, fed some vegetables, cooked the dog, went for a walk on the television, then watched the field for an hour before going to bath. It was time for some new glasses.

or instructions, like this:

I should go and have a break before you start the next section. You will need one teabag, a mug, a little milk, boiling water, and a clear head. Place the teabag in the mug, add the boiling water, remove the teabag, and add the milk. Pour the mixture slowly into your head.

Before you can have a go at sorting out some commas we'd better take a look at the Oxford comma.

You could say,"hammers, knives, guns and facemasks". But you could also say, "hammers, knives, guns, and facemasks". The extra comma before "and" in the second example is called the "Oxford comma". It's not wrong to use it but not many people do any more. Most people think that the "and" between the last things in the list gives enough of a pause by itself.

Where do you think the commas should be in these sentences?

Question 1

Steven forgot to put back into the car the engine the steering wheel the seats and the radio. The owner was surprised disappointed and upset when she came to collect it.

[No comma because it is still one item and hasn't changed into a list yet.]

[beginning of the list]

[list]

Answer 1

Steven forgot to put back into the car the engine, the steering wheel, the seats and the radio. The owner was surprised, disappointed and upset when she came to collect it.

[no need for Oxford comma]

[again no Oxford comma]

Question 2

The shop sold packs of dice cards marbles knives and Jeremy Beadle dolls.

Answer 2

The shop sold packs of dice, cards, marbles, knives, and Jeremy Beadle dolls.

Whether you need a comma after "knives" depends on what you are trying to say. If there is no comma, it would seem that there is one pack which includes knives **and** Jeremy Beadle dolls. This might be a fun pack to have. However, if you mean that there are separate packs for, on the one hand, knives, and, on the other, Jeremy Beadle dolls, you should put the extra comma in after "knives".

An adjective is a word that describes what a thing is like. For example, "green", "tall", "boring" and "beautiful" are all adjectives.

What about lists of adjectives?

The tricky thing is that when you list a number of adjectives that apply to something, sometimes you put in commas and sometimes you don't. For example, some people write:

The long red velvet dress.

and some people write:

The long, red, velvet dress.

Don't worry that this isn't easy. On many occasions doing it either way will be right. But you do have to think about it because there are some times when getting it wrong would look pretty **stupid.** As in:

He was a pretty violent man when confused by commas.

The word "pretty" is used here to mean "fairly" and goes with the "violent" to give a picture of someone who for some reason would get violent when faced with commas he couldn't handle. If you put a comma in the wrong place and said:

He was a pretty, violent man when confused by commas.

it gets a bit strange. For some reason his confusion turns him "pretty" as well as "violent".

Where would you put the commas in these sentences?

Question 1
He looked at the knobbly green wax model of his face and thought how beautiful he was.

Answer 1
He looked at the knobbly green wax model of his face and thought how beautiful he was.
This is fine, but so is "knobbly, green, wax model".

Question 2
The castle was ancient famous airy and close to all local shops.

Answer 2
The castle was ancient, famous, airy and close to all local shops.
We need commas here because it's a list of features.

Question 3
The judge dealt with the matter fairly badly and quickly.

Answer 3
The judge dealt with the matter fairly badly and quickly.
If you put "fairly, badly and quickly' BAAAA! Wr-ong! That would mean that you should read "fairly" and "badly" as two different ways in which the judge dealt with it. But "fairly badly" should be read together – so don't separate the words with a comma.

USING COMMAS TO SET APART THE PEOPLE BEING ADDRESSED FROM THE REST OF THE SENTENCE

It seemed like a good idea at the time, officer.

Here a comma is used to tell you which bit of the sentence is there only to show who is being addressed. So, for example:

The commas show us that the words "ladies and gentlemen" are separate from the rest of the sentence. This makes it easier to understand – just imagine it without the commas. It wouldn't be clear what was going on until you'd got a fair way into the sentence. In the same way:

> Someone, ladies and gentlemen, has been making allegations and I want to know who the alligator is.

> Are you going to meet Jeff, George?

Again, the comma makes it clear that the name at the end is set apart from the rest of the sentence. By having a comma, we know that there are two people in this sentence – Jeff and George. Without a comma, there would only be one – Jeff George. Once again, in a simple sentence, the meaning can be completely changed by missing out that tiny little comma.

See if you can work out what's happened on the next page.

IDIOT'S MISSING COMMA

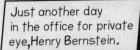

Just another day in the office for private eye, Henry Bernstein.

From: Ian Idiot
To: Henry Bernstein

I want you to meet Lenny Henry. He may have some information on the stolen painting.

Bernstein tracks down Lenny Henry to New York.

This has cost a fortune. I hope Lenny Henry has some good information.

WALK
WALK FASTER

TAXI

Hours later.

I'm terribly sorry, Mr Bernstein, I don't know what you are talking about. Ha ha ha.

Meanwhile back in London.

I wonder what's keeping Bernstein?

LENNY

STOLEN

MR IDIOT

Answer: Mr Idiot's mistake was to write "I want you to meet Lenny Henry" instead of "I want you to meet Lenny, Henry." It's his fault and it's going to cost him a lot of money.

USING COMMAS TO INTRODUCE DIRECT SPEECH

He dived across the beach shouting, "Mine! "Mine!

We'll come back to quoting people later. Just remember for the moment that you can introduce a quotation with a comma.

USING COMMAS TO INTRODUCE QUESTIONS

You are going to give me this video back, aren't you?

One way of asking a question is to make a statement, then add some words which turn it into a question, like "aren't you?" or "won't it?" or "isn't he?" That's nice and straightforward, isn't it?

The person speaking could have said:

> Are you going to give me my video back?

But, by adding the extra bit he has made it clear what answer he expects – he really wants his video back.

USING COMMAS TO EMPHASISE

I started fighting because I felt like it, that's why.

Just like our last example, a comma and an extra bit emphasises what has been said in the rest of the sentence.

USING COMMAS TO BALANCE TWO THINGS THAT ARE BEING COMPARED

The taller they are, the further they have to reach for their shoelaces.

If you imagine that each part of the sentence needs to be balanced, you can see how a comma separates off comparisons.

That's it for commas! Here's a short story to try out your comma skill. See in how many places there should be commas before looking at the answer. I've put in all the other bits of punctuation for you.

Question

It was a beautiful hot summer's day. The friends who had known each other for ten years had been playing all manner of games including rounders boules and volleyball. Although Terry Alderman had wanted to go home they were now playing cricket. He hit the ball high into the air. Joanna Mark Peggy and Sue all looked at each other. Mark spoke up.

"Well I can't catch that can I?" he said. "It's your turn Joanna."

Suddenly a bald man ran across the beach shouting "Duck!" The friends fell to the floor. To their surprise a large white duck flew over their heads with a wig in its beak.

[The information that Terry wanted to go home is separate from the friends playing cricket, so parcel off with a comma.]

[This is just an extra piece of information, so put commas in.]

Answer

It was a beautiful hot summer's day . The friends, who had known each other for ten years, had been playing all manner of games including rounders, boules and volleyball. Although Terry Alderman had wanted to go home, they were now playing cricket. He hit the ball high into the air. Joanna, Mark, Peggy and Sue all looked at each other. Mark spoke up.

[Comma not needed here, but it's a question of style – you might have put one in.]

[a list]

"Well, I can't catch that, can I?" he said. "It's your turn, Joanna."

[a question]

[comma separating out person addressed]

Suddenly a man ran across the beach shouting, [introducing direct speech]

[comma separating two pieces of information]

"Duck!" The friends fell to the floor. To their surprise, a large, white duck flew over their heads with a wig in its beak.

[adjective list]

49

I may be dull, but I think it's particularly important in a subject as difficult as this to summarise things clearly and in a neat way.

COLIN'S CONCLUSIONS PAGE

Commas show a slight pause in the sentence. Don't use a comma just because there is a pause — there may be a better way.

Commas:

   set apart extra information (don't put information in commas if it is needed for the sentence to make sense)

   separate items in a list

   introduce direct speech

   introduce questions

   emphasise

   balance comparisons

50

BRACKETS

Round Ones Looks Like This: ()

You can use brackets to add in an extra comment or fact to a sentence. For example:

Captain Finstaad (who had not seen a shop outside Norway before) was terribly impressed by the Mister Minit shoe-repair stand.

His son (who had travelled the world) was not.

If you took away the words in brackets, both sentences would still make perfect sense. But the information inside the brackets is actually very useful.

That's pretty much all there is to brackets, but you can use them in lots of different ways.

To explain something: The Duke's suicide note (which said, "The gun went off when I was cleaning it") was suspicious.

To add information: His dog (a pedigree poodle) wasn't much of a guard dog.

To add a comment: She was (hardly surprisingly) thrown out of the gang.

To add a reference: Her most telling admission (on page 68 of her book) was that she did goldfish impersonations.

To give examples and paint a picture: That afternoon, his mad activities (including an attempt to bite his own nose) attracted the attention of the mad police.

There are also square brackets which look like this: [ ]

These are not the same as ( ).

For a reason lost in the mists of time people call them "square brackets". Not really. I was just messing about. They're called square brackets because of their shape. They are usually put in by someone who did not write the rest of the sentence, in order to explain or add a comment on it. How about an example?

The person who is quoting this sentence wanted to explain who the "He" was. The square brackets make it clear that the words have been added later by someone else.

Booknews

Mrs Scribble, the manageress of the high street bookshop, said "He [Tim de Jongh] is the author of some fantastic books".

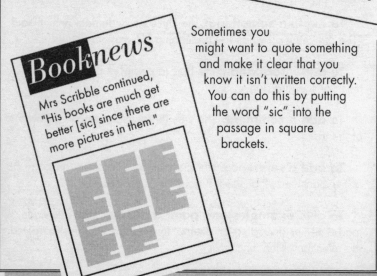

Booknews

Mrs Scribble continued, "His books are much get better [sic] since there are more pictures in them."

Sometimes you might want to quote something and make it clear that you know it isn't written correctly. You can do this by putting the word "sic" into the passage in square brackets.

I accept (and this is a change from my previous view on this) that my clothes are way out of date. Perhaps I need a pair of trendy trainers to impress Zelda.

COLIN'S CONCLUSIONS PAGE

Brackets are useful for adding extra information into a sentence. This can be:

to give an explanation
to give information
to make a comment
to add a reference
to use examples to paint the picture.

53

COLONS
A Colon Looks Like This: :

That's given away the main use of a colon: to introduce something.

Did you know that a large part of your stomach is called your "colon"?

If you find it helpful to think of the comma as something that says, "there will now be a short pause", think of the colon as saying: "Hey, look out everyone! Something's coming!"

These are the things a colon can introduce:

lists
speech and quotations
questions
explanations.

Great! This is an excellent way to remember what it does. I can introduce the following things I like to eat with a colon: cake, chocolate, roast beef and curry.

Good grief! Let's look at that list of things a colon can introduce.

LISTS

This is the most common use of the colon. On the last page you read a list of things a colon can do, set out in "shopping list" form. But when writing sentences it's more usual to set out a list in the following way:

For the lovely "garlic brick" recipe on page 32, you will need the following: water, sand, grit, straw and garlic.

INTRODUCING SPEECH AND QUOTATIONS

We've already seen that you can introduce speech and quotations with a comma. You can also do it with a colon, if you like.

How about this:

Dr. Spock turned to Captain Kirk and said: "There's nothing wrong with him that a small head-removal operation wouldn't sort out."

If you read a play, you'll see the colon is used to introduce speech there, too. For example:

**Steven: What did he just say?
Zelda: I think it was something about colons.
Steven: Oh! Shall we carry on now?**

WARNING

Don't go colon crazy. Sometimes a sentence runs more smoothly without a colon before a list. For example, you shouldn't have a colon in this:

He was the school champion at: English, maths, history, and cheating.

It reads better and makes just as much sense if you do it without the colon, like this:

He was the school champion at English, maths, history, and cheating.

I bet you're asking, "What's the difference between this sentence and the one about the garlic brick?"

Look at the two sentences again.

In the "garlic brick" sentence we're told a list is coming. You can tell that there's almost a drawing in of breath before it starts. The list is a separate thing in itself. The colon says, "Hey, look there's something coming!"

In the "cheating" sentence, there's no real pause in the sense, is there? You could, if you wanted to, rewrite it like this:

He was the school champion in the following subjects: English, maths, history, and cheating.

But it doesn't flow when you read it like that, does it?

QUESTIONS

You can use a colon to introduce a direct question, like this:

The question addressed in Professor Bradshaw's article was simply this: does chocolate milk come from chocolate cows?

EXPLANATION

You can also use a colon to introduce an explanation, like this:

Professor Bradshaw concluded that chocolate milk couldn't come from chocolate cows for one simple reason: the cows would melt in the summer.

Important to remember

1. Don't use capitals after a colon unless the word that follows would have had a capital anyway.

2. Look at the list for the "garlic brick". The first word – "water" – doesn't have a capital. You use a capital only if the word following the colon would have had a capital letter anyway. For example. The football team had three great players: Roy of the Rovers, Mr Shaw and the Queen of England.

On the outside it's the Queen. She passes to Roy of the Rovers...

OK. Anyone who thinks they're a smartypants should try this. Where would you use a colon and where would you use a comma in the following?

Question 1
If there were two things she hated more than being late, they were the following spinach stuck between her teeth without knowing about it and Jeremy Beadle coming to stay.

I think that we're ready to try to spot two things at once.

Oh no we're not!

[introducing the next two things]

Answer 1
If there were two things she hated more than being late they were the following: having spinach stuck between her teeth without knowing about it, and Jeremy Beadle coming to stay.

[Although you could get away without having a comma here, a bit of a pause after the long first item would probably be helpful.]

Question 2
Jackson gave himself away with three tiny errors there was no 7:30 train on a Saturday the uncle's name was not John and he had a badge saying, "I'm the one who stole the painting".

[introducing a list]

Answer 2
Jackson gave himself away with three tiny errors: there was no 7:30 train on a Saturday, the uncle's name was not John, and he had a badge saying, "I'm the one who stole the painting".

[separating the items in the list]

[separating the items in the list]

To impress a girl like Zelda you need to be the following: fashionable, funny and able to sum up things in a clear way.

COLIN'S CONCLUSIONS PAGE

A colon is used to introduce:

lists (do you need a colon or would a list of commas be better?)

quotations (again commas are also possible)

questions

explanations.

SEMI-COLONS

The Semi-Colon Looks Like This: ;

It is made up of a comma and a full stop. Just like them, it marks a pause in a sentence. It is a bigger pause than a comma and a smaller pause than a full stop.

Judging the length of the pause you want is not always easy. After a while you get a feel for it. But until then you can survive without it. So don't get too hung up about it. Still, it is quite fun to have this little mark at the ready. If you know when it can be used, you're less likely to look **stupid** by slipping it in where it shouldn't be.

So, when do you use one?

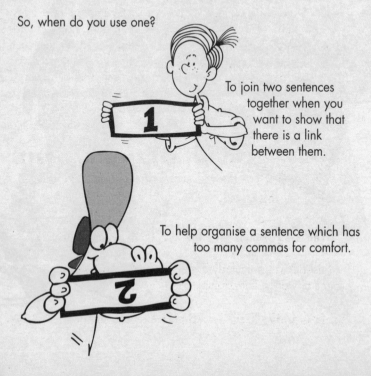

1 To join two sentences together when you want to show that there is a link between them.

2 To help organise a sentence which has too many commas for comfort.

Use a semi-colon instead of a joining word (like "and" or "but" or "because") between two sentences.

A He took the money. He was never seen again.

B He took the money and he was never seen again.

C He took the money; he was never seen again.

1

You can see that in **A** you can use two sentences, in **B** you can use "and" as a joining word, or if you are clever you could use **C** with a semi-colon.

The Why Baby

Whhyyy do you need a semi-colon if you can use other ways to say it?

By having less of a pause than a full stop, you bring the two sentences much closer together and you suggest that the two facts are linked. You could have used "and" but the semi-colon version is a bit punchier, isn't it? Think about that for these examples:

The woman kept coming back to the red car; you could tell she was interested.

The king looked over his subjects; he was quite tall.

This trick is particularly useful when you want to compare the two groups of words. For example:

Tim, who works hard, is rich; Jason, who doesn't, is happy.

WARNING

Use a semi-colon when you want to be dramatic. If you use it too much it will lose its impact and will look **STUPID.**

Also be careful that you use a semi-colon only to link sentences which are complete. If you want a pause in the middle of a sentence, you can either rewrite it or use a dash. For example:

✗ He was a great actor; on most occasions.

Wrong. The "on most occasions" isn't a full sentence. You still might want to have that dramatic pause before "on most occasions". But you can't do it with a semi-colon. So, try it with a dash:

✓ He was a great actor — on most occasions.

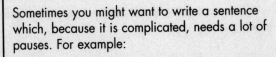

How can semi-colons help my comma confusion?

Sometimes you might want to write a sentence which, because it is complicated, needs a lot of pauses. For example:

The gang had four members: Zelda, a specialist in guns, explosives and welding equipment, Colin, the getaway driver, Steven, the strong man, and Bob Hoskins, who, in something of a mix-up, was on lead guitar.

There are far too many commas, aren't there? It looks ugly and I bet you got lost a couple of times.

You could rewrite it in shorter sentences, like this:

The gang had four members. There was Zelda, who was a specialist in guns, explosives and welding equipment. Colin was the getaway driver. Steven was the strong man. Bob...

Stop! Stop! DULL, DULL, DULL!

What we need is something to show which groups of words go together as one item in the list, and when we're moving on to the next person. The semi-colon comes to the rescue. Look:

The gang had four members: Zelda, a specialist in guns, explosives and welding equipment; Colin, the getaway driver; Steven, the strong man; and Bob Hoskins, who, in something of a mix-up, was on lead guitar.

Did somebody call?

Much easier. Do you see how the semi-colons separate the main groups of words in the list, and the commas are used within each group for more minor pauses?

Now you have a go at putting semi-colons and commas in this one.

Question

The game "Snap" has not been made an Olympic sport for three reasons: it is too fast-moving exciting and skilful for the television cameras it is illegal in certain countries and the President of the Olympic Federation lost his Aunt Edie Uncle Bob and his dog in a tragic card game accident.

Answer

The game "Snap" has not been made an Olympic sport for three reasons: it is too fast-moving, exciting and skilful for the television cameras; it is illegal in certain countries; and the President of the Olympic Federation lost his Aunt Edie, Uncle Bob, and his dog in a tragic card game accident.

Other people might say I have no chance with Zelda; I have yet to introduce her to my milk bottle top collection.

COLIN'S CONCLUSIONS PAGE

The semi-colon is a pause bigger than a comma, but smaller than a full stop.

Semi-colons join sentences together, linking sentences in a dramatic way.

They avoid comma confusion — use the commas to show minor pauses between the major pauses of the semi-colons.

DASHES AND DOTS

The Dash Looks Like This: –
Three Dots Look Like This: ...

First let's look at the dash. This is another punctuation mark which shows a pause in a sentence.

The dash can be used in lots of ways, for example –

Two dashes can be used – like this – as brackets.

A dash can be used to show that something is an afterthought – like this.

A dash can show – er – hesitation and – um – interruption.

A dash can introduce a list – of items, events, feelings or the uses of a dash.

A dash can just indicate a pause – for effect.

We'll go through these ways to use dashes – one by one.

BRACKETS

If you want to include some extra information, dashes work in the same way as brackets. Don't forget that it takes two dashes to parcel off the bit you want to separate.

If you would like an example – and I don't see why you shouldn't have one – then this will do.

Whhyyy use dashes if you could use brackets?

This is one of those style things again. But, if you compare these two sentences, you'll see that dashes give a slightly different effect than using brackets:

He was (thank heavens!) not a Spurs supporter.
He was – thank heavens! – not a Spurs supporter.

Don't you think that the dashes make the "thank heavens!" slightly more involved in the sentence?

AFTERTHOUGHTS

This is probably pretty obvious to you – or anyone else, for that matter.

HESITATION AND INTERRUPTION

Here the dash is particularly helpful if you're writing speech and you want to show that the speakers are being cut off in mid-sentence. Like this:

"I don't know how to say this – "
"What? Are you – "
"Please – let me – in my own way – "
"No! – I'm not listening – "

LISTS

In a list, the dash can be used in the same way as a colon. For example:

The first witch took out the materials — toe of frog, eye of bat, nose of stoat, finger of Whitney Houston, and tongue of spam. The second witch decided she would dial out for a pizza instead.

PAUSES

Like a semi-colon, the dash can join two things together. For example:

"I never thought it was possible to die laughing — until you asked me to marry you," said Zelda to Colin.

But, unlike the semi-colon, the dash doesn't need those two things to be whole sentences. "Until you asked me to marry you" is not a full sentence, but with a dash you can use it anyway.

WARNING

Some people do not like the dash.

Why not – it's nothing to them, surely?

Well, the dash can stand in for a number of other types of punctuation marks, but – and it's a big but – this is one reason it is not popular with some people. Because it can be used so easily, some **stupid** people use it all the time – to try to cover up the fact that they are not sure which other mark to use.

But look at that last paragraph. You can imagine that if you start using the dash too often, your writing might start to look a bit scrappy – breathless – out of control.

So, use it with care, or look

CONTINUING A WORD ON ANOTHER LINE

When you run out of space on your page and you can't fit in a long word, fortun- ately you can use a "-" to finish the word on the next line. Like I just have.

Psst! Want a tip at no extra cost?

Wait a minute, this wasn't mentioned as one of the things a dash does.

Ah, yes, well, there's a reason for that.
As you know, this is a dash: –
This is a hyphen: -

Look similar, don't they?

The difference is that when the "-" occurs half way through a word, we call it a hyphen.

This speaks for itself, but there is one little thing you should know. If you do want to carry on a word on the next line, don't put the dash half-way through one of the syllables (the sounds that make up a word). Put it in the space between the sounds.

For example, don't say that Steven is stupi-
d.

If you really can't fit it on one line, say that he is stupid.

Thank you.

Now let's look at the three dots.

You remember that they look like this:… They are sometimes called a "three dot ellipsis". They show that something has been missed out.

You can use them if you want to use parts of a long quotation but leave other bits out. So, instead of:

Wing Commander Fanbelly wrote, "Of all the many examples of stupid behaviour by the R.A.F., and let me say I am ashamed to admit there has been a very large number of such examples in my short time with the service, I think that trying to fly without wings or any form of power was the stupidest."

You could just put:

Wing Commander Fanbelly wrote, "Of all the many examples of stupid behaviour by the R.A.F.,… trying to fly without wings or any form of power was the stupidest".

This makes it plain to the reader that you have quoted just some of the words he used.

Sometimes, the three dots are used to show that something is left out, with the reader being expected to know what it is. For example:

The R.A.F. has done some stupid things in its time, but trying to fly without wings or any form of power…

Here the writer is saying, "You don't need me to finish this sentence for you, do you?" Or it can be that the three dots just show the passing of time, for example:

"Darling, I don't know how to say this."
He felt a bang on his head, then everything went black…
When he woke up, he was surrounded by people looking at him and making fun of his hair.

Some more examples...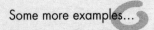

Hold on! This is wrong! Whoever wrote this is **stupid** because thay are trying to show that something is coming up. But as we know, that's the function of the colon or the dash.

Here are some more examples:

Question

Which of the following is wrong?

a   She walked back to the door (if at first you don't succeed...), but then something made her stop.

b   It was just that I thought I might... No, don't bother.

c   The more Peter threw yoghurt at her... the more irritated she became.

Answer

c is wrong, because:

a   The three dots stand for the rest of the saying (try, try, again).

b   The speaker tails off and the rest of the sentence is left unfinished – missed out.

c   Nothing has been missed out here. OK, so you want a pause, but a comma would do just fine.

I think – I'm not sure – Zelda may be washing her hair on the evening I would like to show her my milk bottle tops.

COLIN'S CONCLUSIONS PAGE

Dashes can be used for –
  brackets
  afterthoughts
  introducing a list
  a pause for effect.
        Don't overuse them.

Three dots can be used to:
  show something is missed out
  (eg. in quotations)
  ask the reader to fill in the gap.

Don't use them to introduce things.

APOSTROPHES
An Apostrophe Looks Like This: '

So, does a catastrophe look like this?

Ha, ha, very funny. Now, pay attention.

What you have to remember is that the apostrophe has two very common, but very different, uses.

It can show **possession.** This means that one thing **belongs** to another. For example: Steven's warts. This means that the warts belong to Steven. Lucky Steven!

It can show **omission.** This means that something has been **missed** out. For example, you might write, "Steven's stupid". Written out in full, this would be "Steven is stupid". The apostrophe is to show that the "i" of "is" has been missed out – omitted.

Now, we'll have a look at how each of them works, but first remember this:

Every time you're about to write an apostrophe:

THINK.
Do I want to show possession or omission?
If I don't, I should not be using an apostrophe.

When you have decided that you are showing possession or omission:

THINK.
Where should I put the apostrophe?

STOP

WARNING

Getting the apostrophe wrong is one of those things that drives some otherwise normal people mad.

Possession

NORMALLY

To show ownership, normally you just add an apostrophe and "s" to the thing that is doing the owning, and then write the thing owned. So:

"The spanner of Zelda" becomes "Zelda's spanner".

"The warts of Steven" becomes "Steven's warts".

I'm upset by the "warts". I mean I'm quite fond of them, but shouldn't they have an apostrophe like this: wart's?

Read the first sentence of this section again, Steven. You only add the apostrophe to the thing doing the owning, not the thing owned. The word "warts" has an "s" because there is more than one wart, not because the warts own anything. So no apostrophe.

This isn't just about owning objects, like my spanner, is it?

No, Zelda, good point. You use an apostrophe to show possession of other things too. You could say, for example, "Stephen's lack of understanding was complete".

How would you rewrite the following sentences using the apostrophe?

a The friends of Alison.
b The visiting hours of the local witch-doctor.
c The hairs on my chinny-chin-chin.
d The rules of the apostrophe are less difficult than some people think.
e It was the habit Sheila had of dancing round her handgun that Bruce found so surprising.
f The late goal scored by Arsenal caused the relegation of Norwich City.

Answers

a Alison's friends.
b The local witch-doctor's visiting hours.
c My chinny-chin-chin's hairs.
d The apostrophe's rules are less difficult than some people think.
e It was Sheila's habit of dancing round her handgun that Bruce found so surprising.
f Arsenal's late goal caused Norwich City's relegation.

There is an exception, that is:

Words ending in "S"

Ah ha, I suspected as much!

If the word doing the owning already ends in "s", you have to be a little more careful. There are two rules. What you do depends on whether the word is **singular** (just the one thing, eg. James) or **plural** (more than one thing, eg. boys).

If the owning word is plural, eg. boys, you don't need to add another one. Just add an apostrophe after the "s" that is already there. So:

1

"The bravery of the soldiers" becomes "The soldiers' bravery".
"The hats of the girls" becomes "The girls' hats".

Lots of people get confused and think that the word must have a "s" at the end, or they move the apostrophe, or drop it, or panic and put it everywhere, as in **"The boys' tenni's ball's"** which just looks silly.

Keep calm. Always think about the word doing the owning; in this case, "boy". Before you start adding the apostrophe, is there one or more boy? For example, if you want to say that one boy had some tennis balls, you would write:

The boy's tennis balls.

Because the word doing the owning here doesn't end in "s", it's the normal rule. If you had three boys with tennis balls you would write:

The boys' tennis balls.

I see. So if I discovered that all my warts have hairs, instead of saying "The hairs of my warts", I could say, "My warts' hairs".

Yes, I'm afraid you could, Steven. Oh, dear, how disgusting! What a shame you're still here!

But if I only had one wart, it would be "My wart's hairs".

Shut up, Steven. Shut up. SHUT UP. But you are right, for a change.

If the word is **singular** and ends in "s", eg. James, you add an apostrophe and "s" as normal.

For example: if you wanted to say, "The bicycle of James", you could say "James's bicycle".
If you wanted to say "The neighbours of the Jones family" you could say "The Jones's neighbours".

Ready for the next stage?

Now, one strange thing that you just have to remember. You just have to remember **it**.

It

The word "it" is an exception to the normal rule on possession.

Tell us about it. Sometimes you'll want to say "of it", as in, "The smell of it was awful". If you followed the normal rule of adding an apostrophe and "s" to "it" (the thing doing the owning), you would get:

It's smell was awful.

Don't

Instead, you say "its", without the apostrophe. So:

Its smell was awful.

There is a good reason for this. In the word "it's", the apostrophe only ever shows that something is missing (we'll be looking at this next), so in "It's been lovely to see you", the "It's" is short for "It has". And in "It's a lovely day", the "It's" is short for "It is".

Before we leave this, Zelda, my glamorous assistant, will hold up some important words. These words do not have apostrophes even though they do show possession.

yours, his, hers, ours, theirs, whose

Now your turn. Where would you put apostrophes in this lot?

Question
"Whose football is this?" asked Edwards father.
"Its Bills," said Edward.
"And what is the colour of this football?" thundered Edwards mad Uncle Arthur.
"Its colour is blue," said Edward.
"Speak up, lad!" shouted Arthur, whose hearing was not good.
"Its blue," repeated Edward.
"And whose lawn is this?" the adults voices chimed in together.
"Its the Joness. They have been its owners since 1872," persisted Edward.

[This is short for "It is", so you use the apostrophe.]

[It is the father of Edward, so add and apostrophe and "s" to Edward.]

Answer
"Whose football is this?" asked Edward's father.
"It's Bill's said Edward.

[This is short for "It is the football of Bill" so it's Bill's football.]

"And what is the colour of this football?" thundered Edward's mad Uncle Arthur.

[same as for Edward's father]

[No apostrophe here as this means "of it".]

"Its colour is blue," said Edward.

[exception word]

"Speak up, lad!" shouted Arthur, whose hearing was not good.

[This is short for "It is".]

"It's blue," repeated Edward.
"And whose lawn is this?" the adults'

[The word "adults" ends in "s".]

voices chimed in together.

[short for "it is"]

"It's the Jones's [meaning belonging to the Jones family].
They have been its [Here it means possession.] owners since 1872," persisted Edward.

Omission

Now for something easier.

An apostrophe can also be used to show that something has been left out – omitted. Usually it's when two words have been run together.

Look at the "it's" in the last sentence. It is actually "it is" run together. The apostrophe shows that the "i" in "is" has been dropped.

Quite, and you've put the apostrophe in "it's" correctly as well. Well done.

So when I say "This car's not going to start", the apostrophe in "car's" shows that it's short for "car is", but the "i" is missing.

Here are some more examples:

you will = you'll
that is = that's
can not = can't
you are = you're
does not = doesn't
is not = isn't

we are = we're   of the clock = o'clock
he had = he'd
all is = all's
he will not = he won't
it is = it's

Flashback

Finally, a quick reminder about the apostrophe and "it". You only use "it's" when you mean "it is" or "it has". When you want to show that something belongs to "it" you say "its".

There are lots of examples of this. Can you think of any, Steven?

I've gone blank, sorry. Let's see. I'll try, but I'm not sure it'll come to me in time — it's quite hard.

Six! Very well done!

What?

Oh, never mind.

Hold on before you turn the page. Why do we say "he won't" for "he will not"?

Well spotted – just testing. It looks like a strange exception, but actually it's because "wol" was the old way of saying "will". You don't have to remember that, but you do have to put "won't" and not "willn't".

Can you see what is right and what is wrong with this sentence?

Question

Computer's, which are made of jelly, have proved its true that youll live to be 168 without breathing if you wear a hat made from a sailors ration of peas, despite its unpleasant smell.

Answer

Computers, which are made of jelly, have proved it's true that you'll live to be 168 without breathing if you wear a hat made from a sailor's ration of peas, despite its unpleasant smell.

"Computer's" is wrong because it's just the plural of computer. It's nothing to do with ownership and there's no letter missed out. Also, "you'll" is short for "you will" and so needs an apostrophe. There should be an apostrophe in "sailor's" to show that the ration belongs to a sailor. (If it belonged to lots of sailors it would be "sailors'.") There shouldn't be one in "peas" because it's just a plural. Finally, "its" shouldn't have an apostrophe here as it doesn't mean "it is" or "it has".

Now you know how it works, sit back and have a laugh about how **stupid** this person looked when he just put one tiny apostrophe in the wrong place in this letter.

Dear Cheryl,
My beloved. I have just left Morocco forever. The customs officer forced me to leave my pet dog's behind. It was such a sad moment. It reminded me of the time I had to leave you — and your sad face on the other side of the barrier. Write soon.
Gerhardt.

I've told Zelda that we're going to see a great film about the history of milk bottles. Its title is "Dull Days Indoors".

COLIN'S CONCLUSIONS PAGE

The apostrophe shows:
Possession
Add "s" to the owning word, then put the thing owned, eg. the boy's books.

If the owning word already has an "s":

If it's plural, put the " ' " after the "s" that's already there, eg. the boys' books.

If it's singular, add " 's" as normal eg. James's book.

Remember: an apostrophe shows that something is missing, eg. it's, they'll, we'll, o'clock.

QUOTATION MARKS

Quotation Marks are also called Inverted Commas and Sometimes also Speech Marks
They Look Like This: ' ' (Single) or Like This: " " (Double)

There are two ways in which you can show what someone else has said. You can actually say the exact words that were said. (This is called **direct** speech.) So:

Well, I'm sorry but I would rather stick needles in my eyes than go out with Colin.

would be written as:

"Well, I'm sorry but I would rather stick needles in my eyes than go out with Colin," Zelda told me.

Or you can say what the person meant, by summarising what they said, without actually repeating it word for word. (This is called "indirect" speech – because we are not hearing directly the words that were spoken.) So:

Steven's Diary - Friday 13th
Zelda said that she would rather stick needles in her eyes, than go out with Colin. Zelda said she did not wish to go out with Colin. Zelda apologised, saying that there were other activities which she felt were more appealing than going out with Colin.

As you can see, quotation marks tell us that the words set out between them were the exact words used. This can be useful to tell when we're reading exactly the words that were spoken, and when we have to bear in mind that they are being reported through someone else's choice of words.

How do I show quotes within quotes?

You can use a different pair of quotation marks for the second quote. So if you normally use double quotation marks, you use singles as the inside pair. For example:

He said, "I've had enough of this 'Bill Posters is innocent' campaign."

How do I make it clear who I'm quoting?

You should always make sure it's clear. For example:

The head zookeeper at London Zoo described lions as "the fluffiest little cats on earth".

Look how irritating it is when it is not clear who is speaking:

Michael, Samantha and Barry went to the kitchen. "I think it's time," said Samantha, "to sort out who the killer is." "Who are you looking at?" "Well, it was you standing over the body with a smoking gun in your hand saying, 'Right, that's her shot. Now I'll get the inheritance money', wasn't it?" "OK, so it was me." "I knew it."

Now, whodunnit? I dunnoit.

WHAT EVERYONE GETS CONFUSED ABOUT

It's not so much the quotation marks that people get confused about, as what to do with all the other punctuation marks in the area. Do you put the full stop inside or outside the quotation marks? Where do you put commas? When do you have capital letters?

Don't worry! Here are the answers.

Introducing a Quotation

When you're introducing a quotation, use a comma to indicate the pause between the rest of the sentence and the quoted bit. For example:

He looked her straight in the eye and said, "You've got something in your eye."

Advanced Students Only

You are allowed to use a colon instead.

The quotation here is a complete sentence, and so the quoted bit begins with a capital letter, "Y".

Because it's a complete sentence, that's "Y".

You use the comma in the same way when you want to put the quotation first. Then the pause comes after the quote, for example:

"I'd like a fried potato slice," he said, crisply.

89

And here's another thing to remember when writing down speech.

 "You might have noticed that

each new speaker goes on a new line."

 "You might also have noticed

that each of these "new" lines is

indented."

Finally, you don't have to bother with the comma to introduce the quotation if you're not quoting a full sentence. For example:

> The dentist said my
> teeth were "yellowy and rubbish".

That's it for introducing quotations. The other things that are confusing are interrupting a quotation, and finishing one. We'll move onto them straightaway.

INTERRUPTING A QUOTATION

Sometimes you might want to interrupt a quotation. For example:

"I suppose it's possible," said Mr. Dull, "that the party will be fun without me. I rather doubt it."

Now, do you use a capital letter when you go back to the quotation after interrupting it?

The answer is: it depends on where you've interrupted the quotation.

If you've interrupted it between sentences, you restart with a capital letter.

If you've interrupted it mid-sentence, you carry on as normal with a small letter. So, the above example is correct, and so is:

"I suppose it's possible that the party will be fun without me," said Mr. Dull. "I rather doubt it."

ENDING A QUOTATION

We're now going to look at the bit that really sends people bonkers.

The good news is, it's not that hard. So, by reading the next page and putting in a bit of effort, you can not only avoid looking **STUPID** you can actually look clever instead.

91

The question is always: "Which bits go inside the quotation marks, and which bits go outside?"

The answer is: punctuation marks go inside the quotation marks if they are only to do with the words inside the quotation marks, but outside if they are part of the whole sentence.

Do you remember Mr. Dull's comments about the party? Look back at where the full stops were.

What about this example:

He hissed, "Don't do it!"

The exclamation mark is there to show that the words "Don't do it" are to be given more emphasis than normal. So, as the exclamation mark goes with the words "Don't do it", it goes inside the quotation marks.

If the words "Don't do it" had been said in a normal way, but it was a surprise that they had been said, the exclamation mark would be outside the quotation marks, like this:

To my amazement, he simply said, "Don't do it."!

For a question mark, the same rule applies. For example:

She asked him, "Will you marry me?"

The question is completely within the quotation marks — so the question mark goes within them, too. But how about this:

Did she ask him, "Will you marry me"?

Strictly speaking, this should be:

Did she ask him, "Will you marry me?"?

This is because both the quoted words and the whole sentence are questions.

When this happens, you should put the question mark outside the quotation marks only. So the longer question (that is the whole sentence) gets the question mark and not the smaller one.

I no longer need to say, I may be dull . From now on I will be able to impress with my punctuation.

COLIN'S CONCLUSIONS PAGE

Quotation marks show direct speech.
Always make sure it's clear who's saying what.
Quotes within quotes need a different type of
quotation mark to the ones you usually use.

Introduce a quotation with a comma (or a
colon) before a quote, or a comma within
the quotation marks at the end.

If you interrupt a quotation, the word that
follows the new quotation mark only has a
capital letter if it's a new sentence or if you would
use a capital letter for the first word anyway.

When you end a quotation, put the final bit of
punctuation inside the quotation marks if it
is to do with the words in the quotation,
outside if it completes the whole sentence.

THE FINAL TEST

Now it's time to test you on everything. Get a pen and paper and see if you can write out the following passage, punctuating it correctly.

colin who was a good if dull man was thinking of what zelda might want to do they could have a nights clubbing see colins favourite film or go out for a meal suddenly colin had an idea zelda he said what would you say if i invited you to see my milk bottle collection thats easy said zelda id say no thank you colin its dull

Now check your answer and count up your mistakes.

Colin, who was a good (if dull) man, was thinking of what Zelda might want to do: they could have a night's clubbing; see Colin's favourite film; or go out for a meal.
Suddenly, Colin had an idea. "Zelda," he said, "what would you say if I invited you to see my milk bottle collection?"
"That's easy," said Zelda. "I'd say, "No thank you Colin, it's dull.""

How well did you do?

25 mistakes or more
Well, there wasn't much point you doing it, was there Steven?

20-24 mistakes
Well, you haven't done that well, I'm afraid. Read the book again and you'll do better next time.

15-19 mistakes
Not disastrous at all, because there are a lot of tricky points here, but you should check the bits you got wrong and then have another go.

10-14 mistakes
Better than average - well done! But still not quite good enough. So have another go after looking up the things you got wrong.

5-9 mistakes
Great! Congratulations! You've passed! Turn the page and collect your certificate.

0-4 mistakes
You are either a cheat, or one of the finest punctuators in the country. If it's the latter, turn over and get your certificate now.

The M.O.P. Certificate
(Ministry of Punctuation)

This is to certify that ....

(hereinafter referred to as "the holder of this certificate") can punctuate.

This entitles the holder of this certificate to:

- greater confidence when writing

- more respect from any reader of the writing
of the holder of this certificate

- be a bit uppity with people who can't punctuate

- a fabulous life uninhindered by the nerves and shame
of an inability to punctuate.

Most of all, the holder of this certificate will never, ever look STUPID.

Note this all ye who read.

CONGRATULATIONS!

GRAMMAR
REPAIR KIT

WILLIAM VANDYCK
ANGELA BURT

Illustrated by David Farris

*Hodder
Children's
Books*

a division of Hodder Headline Limited

CONTENTS

For Anna and Matthew, so much more always than mere proper nouns! With all my love, Mum

To Gabriel Gardner, Alexander Vandyck and Joe Firth, who are without exception exceptional. OK boys, listen up. Apart from grammar, there are two things you should know. One is, "It is good to give presents to Uncle William" and the other is something else (I'll let you know when the moment arises). Love, William

INTRODUCTION

GRAMMAR

THE BIG QUESTION: WHY BOTHER?

This is easy.

Try this free quiz:

FREE QUIZ

You write something for an exam, or for a job, or to a friend. For anything. Would you rather seem:

a) not stupid

b) stupid.

Would you prefer people to:

a) understand you?

b) think you are stupid?

OK – aaaaand time's up, stop.

HOW DID YOU DO?

Mostly "b"s. Fine. That's great. You can put this book down and go and play. Or pop into the next room to see if you're there. Or watch some paint dry. Really. Have a good life. Bye! Have you gone yet?

Mostly "a"s. OK. Then you need to know about grammar. Let's leave Stupid ironing his pants and see why.

1

INTRODUCTION

Grammar is about how we put words together to say what we mean.

It's not enough just to know the words you want to use. For a start, you need to know what order to put the words in. You don't say:

Brian buried the octopus. if you mean **The octopus buried Brian.**

What's more, getting the order of the words correct isn't enough if you don't use the right ones. If you want to say:

I read these books while I was on holiday.

you'll look stupid if you actually say:

Me readed them books during me were on holidays.

Finally, getting the wrong word can completely change the meaning of what you say, even if it sounds like it should be OK. For example:

The captain of the ship which was 10 metres wide, carried four aircraft and was made of hard grey steel was smiling.

means:

But

The captain of the ship who was 10 metres wide, carried four aircraft and was made of hard grey steel was smiling.

means:

So, you need to know about grammar. OK?

NOW FOR SOME GOOD NEWS.

We're going to try to avoid using unnecessary jargon. So you won't have to remember about:

the third person singular

the third person plural

the third person's penpal

the third person's poodle

the third person's puddle

the third person's penpal's
poodle paddling in a puddle

And there's some other good news, too...

INTRODUCTION

You are not alone. There's the enormous ghost standing behind you, for a start. Just kidding. Actually, here in the Grammar Repair Kit garage there's Zelda. Say hi, Zelda.

And there's Steven, the Stupid Monster. Say hello, Steven.

Oh, dear. And there's Colin.

Hello. I want to be a teacher, and I'm going to practise on you. Some people say I'm dull. 23 of them. Today, anyway. I keep count, you see, in a little notebook. Well, anyway, I'm really very interesting. Perhaps the most interesting milk-bottle-top collector I know. And I'm going to liven things up with some "jokes" every now and again.

Er, great. I'm sure that's something we're all looking forward to, Colin.

Can I just say I know about Grammar. I see her every Christmas.

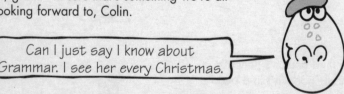

No, Steven, that's Grandma. And anyway, there's no time to say that. We've got to make a start.

Let's go to work.

NOUNS

You've probably heard the term **NOUN** before.
Can you remember what nouns do?

NOUNS are NAMING WORDS. They NAME.

Yes. Like "cleverclogs".

Look around you. Name all the objects you can see. You are using NOUNS.

Name all the people in your class. You are using NOUNS.

Make a list of the presents you would like for your next birthday. You are using NOUNS.

1. spanner 2. engine
3. guitar 4. toolkit

1. present
2. present
3. present

Now, you may wonder ...

Why is it important to KNOW about nouns if I've been using them perfectly well ever since I first learned to talk?

Quite. Well. Colin – help us out here.

Firstly, it's quite interesting.

Secondly, if you know a bit more about nouns then you'll know if they need capital letters or not when you write them and you'll know whether they're singular or plural so that you can make the rest of the sentence match and you'll learn lots of new words.

Thirdly, it helps to know about your own language when you want to learn someone else's like French or German or Italian or Spanish. They have nouns too.

Fourthly, it's the sort of thing your teacher likes you to know about so that you can do well in the National Curriculum tests. So there are lots of reasons, Zelda.

Zelda?

Zelda's off to have fun with words, including nouns. Let's join her.

NOUNS NOUNS NOUNS NOUNS NOUNS

Don't confuse the following:

noun: hat, bird

nun:

nan:

nan bread:

hey nonny no:

In the end, it's like this:

1.   **Person who knows about nouns.**

2.   **Person who doesn't know about nouns.**

You choose.

COMMON NOUNS

Common nouns are the names of objects.

Play "I Spy" for a moment. See how many things you can see beginning with b. All these will be common nouns.

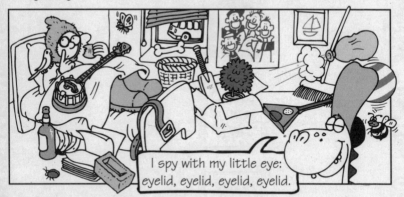

I spy with my little eye:
eyelid, eyelid, eyelid, eyelid.

General words like boy, girl, teacher, parent are common nouns as well.

FIND THE WORDS – WIN A TROPHY!*
(common nouns)

Find ten articles of clothing in this wordsearch:
anorak, boots, gloves, jeans, sandals, scarf, socks, sweater, tie, trousers.

```
T   A   N   O   R   A   K   D
R   I   M   S   O   C   K   S
O   L   E   D   N   F   A   E
U   S   A   N   D   A   L   S
S   C   A   R   F   R   E   P
E   S   E   V   O   L   G   J
R   B   O   O   T   S   K   O
S   W   E   A   T   E   R   Y
```

The answers are all in the back of the book.

* This bit's not true. No trophy. Sorry.

GOING TO THE DOGS: NAME THE BREED
(all common nouns)

1. a l _ _ _ i a n

2. p _ _ _ l e

3. s _ _ _ _ d o g

4. b _ _ _ d o g

5. s _ _ _ i e l

ALPHABET PUZZLE: A IS FOR ARACHNOPHOBE

Think of 26 common nouns, each beginning with a different letter of the alphabet. The zanier your word the better.

a
b
c
d
e
f
g
h
i
j
k
l
m
n
o
p
q
r
s
t
u
v
w
x
y
z

Make sure all the words are common nouns.

There's a musical instrument beginning with xylo . . .

COMPOUND NOUNS:
two for the price of one!!!

Have you ever noticed that some common nouns are really two
nouns joined together? I'm thinking of words like
cupboard, **armchair**, **handkerchief**, **bedroom**, **doughnut**.
We call these **compound nouns** but they're still common nouns
as well.

> I'm a rattlesnake.
> I'm a **compound**
> common noun.

> Yeah, dead
> common, love.

Compound nouns start by being written as two separate words
when they're used together a lot:

a school bus

a washing machine

a pop group

In your lifetime, you'll probably see them begin to be written with a
hyphen. It usually takes years and years before this happens. Some
dictionaries will quickly include them with the hyphen; others will
go on listing them in the old two-word way.

In my dictionary, these compound nouns are now listed with a hyphen:

taxi-driver

motor-bike

crash-helmet

Eventually, they'll probably be written as single words.
Or, if you're reading this in the year 2090 – "singlewords".

Check in your dictionary how these words are written:

hair brush	hair-brush	hairbrush
table cloth	table-cloth	tablecloth
shop keeper	shop-keeper	shopkeeper
head ache	head-ache	headache
fire guard	fire-guard	fireguard

COLIN'S CONCLUSIONS PAGE

= pancake

Look Steven, if you can't work out where "pancake" comes from within another 15 seconds, I'm going to suggest we move on to "peabrain".

PROPER NOUNS

Proper nouns are the individual names of people, pets, towns, countries, clubs and organisations, and so on. They always begin with a capital letter.

COMMON NOUNS	PROPER NOUNS
girl	Kayleigh
town	Exmouth
dog	Bonzo

I'm **Colin** (proper noun). I am a **boy** (common noun). I want to be a **teacher** (common noun).

That's quite enough of that, **idiot** (common noun)!

Make your answers start with a capital S-s-s-s-s-s.

IT'S ONLY PROPER, INNIT?

1. Name a country.   S_____

2. Name a town.   S_____

3. Name a planet.   S_____

4. Name a mountain.   S_____

5. Name a river.   S_____

6. Name a girl.   S_____

7. Name a boy.   S_____

HUNT THE PROPER NOUNS

Find the five nouns which are proper nouns and write them out properly with a capital letter at the beginning.

manchester   pencil

    doctor   village   wales

chicken   brian   basket

      norway   everest

crisps   road

1. _____
2. _____
3. _____
4. _____
5. _____

GENERAL KNOWLEDGE QUIZ

1. Who wrote 'James and the Giant Peach'?

2. What was Shakespeare's first name?

3. What's the capital of Sweden?

4. Which Germanic god is Thursday named after?

5. Which month has 28 days? ***

*** Watch out! Question 5 is a ...

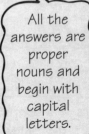

All the answers are proper nouns and begin with capital letters.

COLLECTIVE NOUNS

Collective nouns are the names of collections of things like a **herd** of cows, a **bouquet** of flowers, an **anthology** of poems, a **swarm** of bees.

COLLECTIVE STRENGTH TEST

Do you know the missing collective nouns?

1. a _____ of sheep
2. a _____ of ships
3. a _____ of stars
4. a _____ of fish
5. a _____ of thieves

You can have fun making up collective nouns. We haven't got enough in the language!

MAKE UP YOUR OWN COLLECTIVE NOUNS – WIN A TROPHY*

1. a _____ of teachers
2. a _____ of skeletons
3. a _____ of bicycles
4. a _____ of pop groups
5. a _____ of computers

a **cuddle** of kittens

a **squelching** of tadpoles

a **wetness** of kisses

a **hatstand** of hatstands

a **problem** of bad breath

* *Not true here, either. Sorry.*

GENERAL UNDERSTANDING

MAJOR POINT

Now pay attention to this next bit. It's quite complicated. Carry on, Major Point.

COLLECTIVE NOUNS ARE SINGULAR (unless you make them plural).

Here is an example.

You should say: a **swarm** of bees **has** landed on Colin's head. ✓

You shouldn't say:
a **swarm** of bees **have** landed on Colin's head. ✗

I agree.

If you like, you can make **swarm** plural. You can change it into **swarms**. Then you can say "have landed".
Swarms of bees **have** landed on Colin's head.

No, don't say that! Help!

YOU STOP

IT'S TIME TO TEST YOUR UNDERSTANDING!

TEST YOUR UNDERSTANDING OF THIS VERY ADVANCED GRAMMATICAL POINT

1. A herd of cows _____ eating your lawn. Ha ha! (is/are)

2. A bouquet of flowers _____ presented to the winner of the "Don't kill flowers" competition. (was/were)

3. That suite of furniture _____ too bouncy to be safe. (is/are)

4. Crowds of fans _____ at the concert. (was/were)

5. A large crowd of supporters _____ shouting slogans.(was/were)

We only sing when we're singing. Sing when we're singing...

AND NOW HEAR THIS:

You are the secretary of the General, who isn't quite sure which words to use where he has put alternatives. Can you say which words is/are correct – by teatime?

MEMO TO TROOPS:

The army which is/are going on these missions should be aware that they will be dangerous. Neither success, nor glory, nor a filling packed lunch is guaranteed. It may very well be that this brave troop is/are unlikely to want to go if there is no packed lunch. I understand. But anyone in this army who is not willing to go just for that reason should give his or her name to me and I will try to cadge some sandwiches and cubes of cheese and Penguin biscuits for them.

I would wish to make sure that this rabble realise/realises that the whole thing is not just about food, you know. Many have mentioned this issue to me. But if just a few of you were more interested in getting out there and fighting rather than stuffing your faces all the time, I wouldn't be known as "Lardyguts" Understanding at the club.

Yours **General "Lardyguts" Understanding**

ABSTRACT NOUNS

Abstract nouns are the names of feelings, thoughts and concepts. You can't hold them in your hand. You can't smell them. You can't hear them or see them.

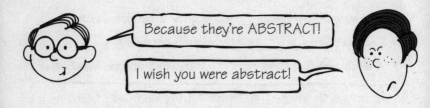

Because they're ABSTRACT!

I wish you were abstract!

Here are some abstract nouns.

kindness	sympathy
affection	love
fear	freedom
childhood	generosity

Abstract nouns have a lot of different endings. Here are some of them:

-ness	-dom	-ty	-ion	-ice
-hood	-our	-ship	-ment	-ure

Choose the right ending for these abstract nouns.

1. friend _____
2. nervous _____
3. boy _____
4. king _____
5. loyal _____
6. excite _____
7. just _____
8. fail _____
9. cruel _____
10. gentle _____

Sometimes abstract nouns are quite difficult to spell because you don't just have to add an ending. You have to change the word in other ways as well.

For example:

high	height
wise	wisdom
silent	silence
sincere	sincerity

You'll get to know the common ones. Use a dictionary if you're not sure.

TESTING TESTING ONE TWO THREE FOUR.
OH, YOU GET THE GENERAL IDEA.

Change these words into abstract nouns.

1. lonely   ness
2. miserable   y
3. confident   ce
4. generous   ity
5. cowardly   ice
6. lazy   Actually, don't bother with this one.

Fill in the missing letters in these abstract nouns.

7. proud   pr _ _ _
8. wide   wi _ _ _
9. brave   brav _ _ _
10. noble   nob _ _ _ _ _
11. beautiful   b _ _ _ _ _

GENERAL POINTS ABOUT NOUNS

GENDER

Nouns are said to be masculine if they refer to males. When are nouns said to be masculine, Steven?

When they refer to males.

Correct, for example: **boy**, **father**, **uncle**, **stallion**, **cockerel**.

Nouns are said to be feminine if they refer to females. When are nouns feminine, Steven?

When they refer to females.

That's right – **girl**, **mother**, **aunt**, **mare**, **hen**.

Nouns are said to be common if they refer to both male and female. When are they said to be common?

When they refer to both male and female.

Right – eg **child**, **parent**, **relation**, **horse**, **fowl**.

Don't confuse this meaning of the word "common" with "common nouns" as explained on page 8.

Nouns are said to be neuter if they refer to objects: **pen**, **table**, **fork**, **spoon**.

When are nouns said to be neuter, Steven?

When they refer to objects.

Yeah. Steven is said to be stupid if he asks, "When do I get a pie in my face?"

When do I get a pie in my face?

Now!

GENDER-AL KNOWLEDGE

Sort these nouns into the four gender columns (masculine, feminine, common and neuter).

nun   chair   nephew   judge   ram   book

telephone   bull   heiress   doctor   desk   daughter

grandfather   pet   queen   teacher

STAND-INS

Find words of common gender that can take the place of these masculine and feminine nouns:

1. headmistress

2. clergyman

3. foreman

4. policeman

5. spokesman

YOU DON'T HAVE TO KNOW THIS BUT...

Listen out for people referring to things like cars or ships as if they were female.

She's been a wonderful ship, and never let me drown before.

She's a bit old and battered, bad at starting in the morning and high-maintenance, but the car's OK.

SINGULAR AND PLURAL

Singular means ONE of something.

Plural means MORE THAN ONE.

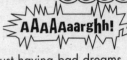

AAAAAaarghh!

It's OK, Zelda, you were just having bad dreams.

Be careful with the spelling when you make
nouns plural. This is the general rule:

MOST WORDS ADD -S OR -ES TO FORM THE PLURAL.

But, yes, you've guessed it. That's not the end of the story.
And you know what they say, the story ain't over till the fat lady sings.

You mean isn't.

La!

CLEVER TROUSERS

Not yet, Fat Lady – do try to pay attention.

Oh, sorry, there's more about
plurals than just adding -s or -es,
isn't there?

Yes Ye-s Y-es!

Nouns ending in -y

Nouns ending in vowel +y add -s

(e.g. monkey monkeys)

Nouns ending in consonant +y change the y to i before adding -es

(e.g. lady ladies)

Nouns ending in -o

Nouns ending in -o usually add -s but there are some important exceptions like potato**es** and tomato**es**.

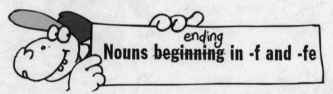

Nouns ~~beginning~~ ending in -f and -fe

Nouns ending in -f and -fe usually add -s but sometimes you have to remember to change the f to v (as in half – hal**v**es and wife – wi**v**es) before adding –**e**s.

And there are still more irregular plurals to remember.

Regular soldier

Irregular soldier

PECULIAR PLURALS

man	men
child	children
woman	women
mouse	mice
louse	lice

EVEN MORE PECULIAR PLURALS

goose	geese
tooth	teeth
foot	feet

GETTING VERY ODD NOW

cod	cod
trout	trout
salmon	salmon
sheep	sheep
deer	deer

STEADY I THINK SHE'S GONNA BLOW

oasis	oases
radius	radii
bacterium	bacteria
antenna	antennae

LOOK OUT EVERYBODY!

syllabus	syllabi or syllabuses
terminus	termini or terminuses

TRANCEOMETER

110
Colin says
something
interesting.

80
Dog sumo
wrestler
sues man.

60
Dog
sues
man.

40
Man
bites
dog.

20
Dog
bites
man.

AND... RELAX:

If the plural is irregular
(i.e. peculiar)
it will be in your
dictionary.

**So remember to look up spellings you're not
sure about.**

FIND THE PECULIAR PLURALS –
OR YOUR FAVOURITE THING EXPLODES

Yes! We've placed a tiny computerised bomb in your – yes, your, Mr/s (delete as appropriate) .... (put name here) favourite thing. It will go off in one minute from now, unless you find all six words with peculiar plurals in this wordsearch puzzle. There are two words in the singular – can you say what their plurals should be?

```
E   S   E   E   G   E   N
S   E   M   R   E   E   D
U   S   A   L   M   O   N
O   A   N   O   C   E   E
M   O   W   T   E   E   F
```

Zelda – you're a singular kind of girl. Why don't I give you a ringular later, and we'll go out and do somethingular.

Colin – go and work out the plural of "No".

Nose?

USING THE POSSESSIVE APOSTROPHE

There is a strange, bad-tempered breed of monster called a Rophe.

One particular breed of Rophe likes crawling through people's letterboxes when they're eating breakfast. This breed was originally known as "a Post Rophe".

However, language has developed over the years (see page 10), and these monsters are now known as

APOSTROPHES.

And when people say that they don't know how to deal with an apostrophe (pronounced a-poss-tra-fee) it must be the little monster that looks like that that they're thinking about.

Because dealing with the apostrophe that looks like this ' is really easy when you know how!

You want to show that Zelda owns the spanner?
Is it:

> Zeldas spanner? Zeldas' spanner?
> Zelda's spanner? Zeldas s'panner?
>
> I know, I'll lie. I'll say it's someone else's.

No, you don't need to lie. The good news is there's a really easy way to get it right...

NOUNS

Stanley Savenergy's Ruler:

Of course he saves energy: I do the measuring for him.

Stanley Savengery's Rule:

1. Name the owner.   Zelda

2. Put the apostrophe next.   Zelda'

3. If there isn't an s immediately
   before the apostrophe, add one.   Zelda's

4. Add the rest.   Zelda's spanner

Use it safely with plural words too, whether they're peculiar plurals or not. Sometimes you'll end up with s' and sometimes with 's. Everything will sort itself out if you follow the rule.

The cries of the babies

Name the owner.	babies
Put the apostrophe next.	babies'
If there isn't an s, add one.	(already got an s)
Add the rest.	babies' cries

The books of the children

Name the owner.	children
Put the apostrophe next.	children'
If there isn't an s, add one.	children's
Add the rest.	children's books

COLiN'S CHALKBOARD CONCLUSiONS

NOUNS

1. Nouns are naming words.

2. There are four kinds of nouns: common, proper, collective and abstract.

3. Nouns can be masculine, feminine, neuter or common gender.

4. Most nouns form their plural by adding -s or -es (but BE CAREFUL!).

5. Possessive apostrophes are put directly after the owner's name.

This is an announcer.

This is a noun, sir.

JUST
MESSING ABOUT

Time to have a break!

Let's have some useless interesting information.

Tell us about eponyms.

EPONYM: the person that something is named after.

Example: Julius Caesar who gave his name to July.

Can you guess what was named after the following six people?

1. Jean Nicot (1530-1600), French diplomat, first introduced tobacco to France.

Not to be confused with Nick O'Tel, the famous hotel thief of the 1860s.

2. American president Theodore Roosevelt (1858-1919), nicknamed Teddy, once spared the life of a bear cub while out hunting.

Er... I will spare you.

3. Joseph Guillotin (1738-1814) gave his name to a machine which was used to behead people during the French Revolution.

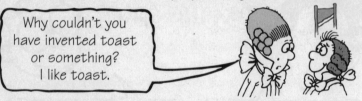

Why couldn't you have invented toast or something? I like toast.

4. Laszlo Biro (1900-1985), Hungarian inventor, made a pen with quick-drying ink which worked better at high altitudes than ordinary fountain pens and was used by the RAF during World War Two.

Can I borrow your Laszlo?

5. Lord Sandwich (1718-1792) was a dreadful gambler who begrudged time wasted at the dinner table. He preferred to eat a snack while he carried on gambling, usually a slice of beef between two slices of bread.

Actually there's another theory about that.

6. Joseph Cyril Bamford (b.1916) developed and manufactured an earth-moving machine with a huge scoop in the front operated hydraulically.

Look what I've invented, Mr B.U.L.L. Dozer.

Bah, now I'll never be famous.

PRONOUNS

Read this very boring letter written by one of Colin's friends.
(Actually it is so boring that we'll just ask you to read one page.)

> and then Zelda and Steven asked Colin if Colin would like
> Zelda and Steven to paint Colin a picture. Colin said that
> Zelda and Steven were very kind to offer to paint a picture
> for Colin but Colin was actually very good at painting and
> Colin thought that Colin could probably paint a better
> picture than Zelda and Steven could. Zelda and
> Steven were upset.

Wasn't that REALLY REALLY boring! It would be a bit better if all
that Zelda and Steven and Colin stuff could be cut down.

And it CAN! This is where PRONOUNS come in. Pronouns can do
the work of nouns by standing in for them.

> and then Zelda and Steven asked Colin if <u>he</u> would like <u>them</u>
> to paint <u>him</u> a picture. Colin said <u>they</u> were very kind to
> offer to paint a picture for <u>him</u> but <u>he</u> was actually very
> good at painting and <u>he</u> thought that <u>he</u> could probably paint
> a better picture than <u>they</u> could. <u>They</u> were upset.

Sure, it's still pretty dull (I did say it was a friend of Colin's), but at
least your head won't start to spin when reading it. The pronouns
that we've used here to replace the proper nouns Zelda, Steven
and Colin are personal pronouns. They are called personal
pronouns because they mostly refer to people.

I'm pro-bananas.

UP ME!

I'm pro-noun.

33

PERSONAL PRONOUNS

I	you	he	she	it	we	they

me	you	him	her	it	us	them

Personal pronouns come in pairs.

How do you know whether to use the one in the top box or the one in the bottom box?

It's easy.

Look at this example: **Zelda** kicks the ball.

Zelda is DOING the kicking. She is a DOER. Use a pronoun from the top box.

She kicks the ball.

Now look at this example: Colin kicks **Zelda**.

Zelda (poor thing!) is having the kicking DONE to her. Use a pronoun from the bottom box.

Colin kicks **her**.

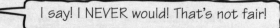
I say! I NEVER would! That's not fair!

That's true. Let's think of a more likely example.

They kicked **him.**

CHOOSE THE RIGHT PRONOUN

1. My little brother is always annoying (I / me).
2. (We / us) love cooking.
3. My uncle didn't recognise (I / me).
4. (They / Them) collect spiders.
5. (She / Her) loves all animals.

A DIFFICULT BIT MADE A BIT LESS DIFFICULT

Some people find it very difficult deciding whether to use I or me in sentences like this:

My mother and ___ love chocolate.

The best thing to do is to think of it as two sentences before you make up your mind.

My mother loves chocolate.
I love chocolate.

My mother and **I** love chocolate. ✓

Here's another example:

The Queen has invited my friend and _____ to tea.

The Queen has invited my friend to tea.
The Queen has invited **me** to tea.

The Queen has invited my friend and me to tea. ✓

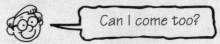

Can I come too?

No. This method works in sentences like this too.

The invitation has been given to you and _____.
The invitation has been given to you.
The invitation has been given to **me**.
The invitation has been given to you and **me**. ✓

CHOOSE I OR ME IN THESE SENTENCES

1. My friend and (I / me) are very sorry.
2. Let my friend and (I / me) off this time so we can do it again.
3. Please invite Sarah and (I / me) to your party. We do so want to snub you by not coming.
4. You and (I / me) will teach the bullies to crawl.
5. They'll have to crawl in order to get you and (I / me) out from under the bed.

"We don't tend to have this problem."

35

POSSESSIVE PRONOUNS

mine   yours   his   hers   ours   theirs

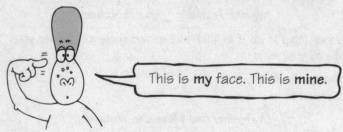

This is **my** face. This is **mine**.

Possessive pronouns show who owns something. They're easy to use BUT there is one important thing you have to remember.

POSSESSIVE PRONOUNS DON'T NEED APOSTROPHES.

Quite right, Colin. Pronouns don't need them. They speak for themselves.

So you never write "your's" or "our's". No.

PUT THAT BISCUIT DOWN AND CHECK YOU UNDERSTAND THIS NOW, OK?

Use possessive pronouns instead of the underlined words.

1. That's <u>his lunchbox</u> not <u>your lunchbox</u>.
   That's _____ not _____.

2. The car was <u>their car</u> but now it's <u>my car</u>.
   The car was _____ but now it's _____.

Possessive pronouns speaking for themselves

Whose was the least successful team in the world?

Theirs.

REFLEXIVE PRONOUNS

Oh Colin! Have you hurt **yourself**?

Yes, the phone rang and it was a reflex action. I found I was ironing myself.

myself   yourself   himself   herself   itself
ourselves   yourselves   themselves

These pronouns are called reflexive pronouns. Colin thinks that they should be called "boomerang" pronouns because they always refer back to the DOER.

I wash **myself**.

You hurt **yourself**.

They dress **themselves**.

Be careful with the spelling. Don't make the mistakes that Steven makes.

ourselfs x
yourselfs x
theirselfs x
themselfs x

I haven't shown myself in the best light, have I?

You'll have to educate yourself.

Don't use **myself** when you need **I** or **me**.

My friend and ~~myself~~ like ice-cream.
My friend and **I** like ice-cream.

They invited my friend and ~~myself~~.
They invited my friend and **me**.

38

COLIN'S CHALKBOARD CONCLUSIONS

PRONOUNS

1. Pronouns take the place of nouns.

2. Personal pronouns come in pairs. Be careful to choose the right one of the pair.

3. Possessive pronouns don't need apostrophes.

I "pronoun"ce you "she" and "he".

How do you pronounce "He is Dull"?

I give up, how do you pronounce "He is Dull?"

Never mind.

JUST MESSING ABOUT

Let's have a break! We're EXHAUSTED!

Good idea! Let's take a break and find out where some of the words in our language come from.

break: a pause for rest   (Old English <u>brecan</u> = to break)

exhausted: tired out   (Latin <u>exhaustus</u> = drained dry)

Can you match up these words with where they have come from? The first one is done for you.

bungalow   Hindustani – leg clothing

dandelion   Spanish – a courtyard

dinghy   Italian – little strings

ketchup   Italian – little worms

khaki   Urdu + Persian – dusty

patio   Hindi – a small boat

pyjamas   Old English – a spinner

robot   French – lion's teeth

spaghetti   Hindi – Bengal thatched house

spider   Czech – compulsory labour

terminus   Hindi – robber, murderer

thug   Malay – fish sauce

vermicelli   Latin – end, limit

If you get stuck, your dictionary will help you.

40

ADJECTIVES

Adjectives are describing words. They help to make a description lively and detailed.

They describe nouns:

The man had guns.

Bit dull, eh? Look how much more interesting things are when you add adjectives.

The bad man had big guns.

And look how important adjectives can be.

The bad man had big broken guns.

They can describe pronouns, too.

TIME FOR SOME FUNKY WORK

Describe a friend

List five adjectives that describe your best friend.

Stamp out the evil intruder

Cross out the word in each line which is NOT an adjective.

1. happy   tall   bed   miserable
2. delicious   apple   green   early
3. across   sad   young   lazy
4. lonely   small   expensive   car
5. empty   myself   sunny   rich

Add an adjective

Add ten adjectives that will make this description more interesting.

The wind was _____. The night was _____.

The children were _____ as they trudged along

the _____ path through the wood. They

wished they were at home, _____ and

_____ in front of a _____ fire.

We asked two famous people and Colin to add their choice of adjectives to show how much difference it can make.

Look ➡

ALL THE DIFFERENCE IN THE WORLD

Enid the Nice Aunty

The wind was **nice**. The night was **warm**.
The children were **happy** and **cosy** as they trudged along the
lovely and **nice** path through the **pretty** wood. They wished they
were at home, **nice** and **happy** in front of a **pretty**, **cosy** fire.
And soon they were!

Mike the Horror Writer

The wind was **scary**. The night was **icy** and **cold**.
The children were **barefoot**, **tired**, **hungry**, **miserable**,
diseased and going **green** as they trudged along the **evil** path
through the **haunted** wood. They wished they were at home,
safe and **uninjured** in front of a **real** fire. Instead of fires of
Hell, which now awaited.

Yes, all right Mike, steady on.

Colin

The wind was **light** to **steady**. The night was **normal**.
The children were **normal** as they trudged along the **straight**
path through the **wooded** wood. They wished they were at home
average and **normal** in front of a **guarded** fire. The End.

FIVE KINDS OF ADJECTIVES

ADJECTIVES OF QUALITY

All the adjectives we've used so far have been adjectives of quality.
They're fun to use because they add vivid and interesting details.
Look at this dull sentence:

The dog has teeth.

Now add some adjectives of quality telling us what the teeth are like:

The dog has **huge yellow** <u>teeth</u>.

Use adjectives when you write to make your descriptions come to life.

DEMONSTRATIVE ADJECTIVES:

this   that   these   those

Demonstrative adjectives are "pointing out" adjectives:
that <u>bus</u>, **those** <u>computers</u>, **this** <u>book</u>, **these** <u>pens</u>.

That <u>dog</u> has yellow teeth.

Look at **those** <u>teeth</u>.

Can you see now why it is ungrammatical to say "them teeth"?

Them is a pronoun.

Colin is right. You need the demonstrative adjective "those", not the
personal pronoun "them".

Pronouns can't describe nouns.

ADJECTIVES OF QUANTITY

All the numbers (**one**, **two**, **three** ... and **first**, **second**, **third** ...)
are adjectives when they are used to describe nouns and pronouns.

These adjectives can add precise useful detail too.

The dog has **fifteen** huge yellow <u>teeth</u>.
The **first** <u>time</u> I saw them I was terrified.

Always write numbers as words when they are being used as adjectives.

SPELLING QUIZ

Write these numbers as words:

15 _____   40 _____

90 _____   5th _____

8th _____   12th _____

Check your answers at the back of the book – how did you do,
and what does it say about you?

7 or more: You are a liar and a cheat. There are only
6 questions.

6: Top marks – congratulations! Give yourself a chocolate and a
pat on the head, allow yourself to be carried around shoulder high
and mugged by autograph hunters for a bit... then carry on.

4-5: Pretty good; you're OK, you know? Just check those you got
wrong, then move on.

1-3: Oops! Don't be too hard on yourself, though. Don't forget
even... (insert the name of your favourite person here) ..... couldn't
spell these words at one stage in his/her life. Go through them till
you get them right, then go on.

0: Bad luck, Steven.

POSSESSIVE ADJECTIVES:

my   your   his   her   its   our   their

Possessive adjectives show ownership.

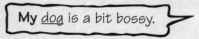

My <u>dog</u> is a bit bossy.

Other dogs wag **their** tails. My dog wags **its** finger at me.

Notice that you DON'T need any apostrophes.

its – possessive adjective
it's – short form of it is / it has

INTERROGATIVE ADJECTIVES

These adjectives can begin questions by describing a noun.

Whose <u>dog</u> is this?

Colin's — don't you pay
attention to anything?

What <u>subject</u> do you like best?

Which <u>film</u> did you see?

Which film?

Witch film

OUR NEW COMPETITION: SPOT THE SPOTS

SPOT THE DIFFERENCE:

whose – interrogative adjective
who's – short form of <u>who</u> <u>is</u> / <u>who</u> <u>has</u>

SPOT TEST:

1. _____ been eating my porridge?

2. _____ bicycle is that?

3. _____ mother can play the trumpet?

4. _____ coming to your party?

5. _____ penfriend lives in Germany?

SPOT CHECK:
its and it's

1. The butterfly spread _____ wings.

2. My cup has lost _____ handle.

3. _____ a lovely day today.

4. Smell that rose. _____ scent is wonderful.

5. _____ taken the five hours to find you.

SPOT THE DOG:

It's me again!

47

COMPARISON OF ADJECTIVES

BIG BIGGER BIGGEST

Add **-er** and **-est** to short adjectives to make comparisons.

Zelda is **tall** for her age. (positive)
Colin is **taller** than Zelda. (comparative)
Steven is **tallest** of all. (superlative)

ATTENTION!

Notice the spelling changes in some of these words.

short	shorter	shortest
sad	sadder	saddest
brave	braver	bravest
heavy	heavier	heaviest

Use **more** and **most** with longer adjectives

difficult	more difficult	most difficult
mysterious	more mysterious	most mysterious
intelligent	more intelligent	most intelligent
loving	more loving	most loving

Use **less** and **least** to go in the other direction.

difficult	less difficult	least difficult
mysterious	less mysterious	least mysterious
intelligent	less intelligent	least intelligent
loving	less loving	least loving

Remember these peculiar ones:
good better best
bad worse worst

YES
Now you can get your words in three different strengths!
NEW NEWER NEWEST
formula

REMEMBER

- Use the comparative when you are comparing TWO people or things.

Zelda is **more beautiful** than Colin.
Zelda is **smaller** than Colin.

- Use the superlative when you are comparing THREE or more.

Zelda is the **most beautiful** of all.
Zelda is the **smallest**.

AND REMEMBER:

Never muddle up the two ways of forming the comparative.

Never muddle up the two ways of forming the superlative.

Steven is the most kindest monster I have ever met.   ✗

Apples are more nicer than pears.   ✗

Zelda is more beautifuller than you.   ✗

Steven is the kindest monster I have ever met.   ✓

Apples are nicer than pears.   ✓

Zelda is more beautiful than you.   ✓

And so:

Good man   **Comparatively Better Man**   **SUPERLATIVEMAN**

DID YOU KNOW?

Did you know that proper nouns are sometimes used as adjectives to describe other nouns?

A **London** <u>park</u>
A **Paris** <u>slum</u>

Did you know that some adjectives have been made from proper nouns and still keep their capital letters?

An **English** <u>accent</u>
A **German** <u>car</u>

Did you know that common nouns are sometimes used as adjectives?

A **glass** <u>bottle</u>
A **grass** <u>skirt</u>
A **garden** <u>gnome</u>

Did you know that a group of words can do the work of an adjective?

A **happy-go-lucky** <u>smile</u>
A **don't-disturb-me-now** <u>frown</u>
A **milk-white** <u>lily</u>

Give me your <u>butter-wouldn't-melt-in-my-mouth</u> smile!

You are not just stupid. You are not just more stupid than other things like rocks and stones. You are the stupidest thing since Mr Stupid did a stupid thing stupidly.

COLIN'S CHALKBOARD CONCLUSIONS

ADJECTIVES

1. Adjectives describe nouns and pronouns.
2. When numbers are used as adjectives, always write them as words.
3. Don't say: look at them teeth. You need an adjective, not a pronoun.
   ✓ Look at those teeth.
4. Possessive adjectives don't need apostrophes.
5. Use the comparative form when comparing two things.
6. Use the superlative form when comparing three things or more.

Dynamic
Useful
Lovely
Likeable

Which of these words do you think best describes me?

That one.

DULL

JUST MESSING ABOUT

AMERICANISMS

If an American friend offers you a bag of chips, might they come wrapped in newspaper? No, definitely not! Americans call them chips, but we call them crisps.

If your friend offered you candy, what would you expect? Yes, sweets.

How many of these Americanisms can you "translate" into British English? You'll find the answers in the back of the book if you get stuck on any.

American English

1. cookies
2. checkers
3. comforter
4. crosswalk
5. deck (of cards)
6. diaper
7. elevator
8. the fall
9. faucet
10. fender (of a car)
11. garbage can
12. gas
13. hood (of a car)
14. overpass
15. pacifier
16. pants
17. purse
18. sidewalk
19. stroller
20. trunk (of a car)

British English

fender

pants

sidewalk

trunk (of a car)

checkers

deck (of cards)

the fall

VERBS

Verbs are DOING words and also BEING words.

DOING WORDS

Colin **saves** the ball.

Colin **swam** all the way to France.

Colin **drives** very fast and fantastically.

BEING WORDS

Colin **is** a big fibber about all of those things.

Colin **feels** a bit stupid now I've told you.

Their son **grew** very tall.

THE PRESENT TENSES

Verbs can show things happening in the past, in the present and in the future.

If you want to describe something happening NOW, you have three present tenses to choose from.

> I **shout** at Zelda.
>
> I **am shouting** at Zelda.
>
> I **do shout** at Zelda.

They each mean something very slightly different. You have to choose the one that fits your meaning best.

The first example means that I shout at Zelda and then stop.

The second example means that I am in the middle of shouting at Zelda.

The third example is a confession that I shout at poor Zelda rather a lot!

If you want to ask a question, you have to use the last two tenses.

Am I shouting at Zelda?

Do I shout at Zelda?

If you want to give an order, you have to use the first and the last.

Shout at Zelda!

Do shout at Zelda!

Do shut up!

ROADSIDE CHECK

Circle the verbs in these sentences:

1. I hate cabbage and sprouts.
2. Steven punched Colin on the nose.
3. You are silly.
4. My dog eats vegetables.
5. We bought some fireworks.
6. Swallow your medicine.

Now let's have a bit of a rest before we talk about past tenses.

Did you know that some words can be used as nouns (naming words) and verbs (doing and being words)?
Here is an example: **shout**

Give a loud **shout**. (noun)
Shout loudly. (verb)

Oh don't start shouting again!

TEST YOUR UNDERSTANDING

Make up two sentences for each word (write your answers on a separate sheet of paper).
In the first sentence, use the word as a noun.
In the second sentence, use the word as a verb.

1. kiss
2. work
3. help
4. dream
5. walk

DICTIONARY WORK

Use your dictionary to help you make these nouns and adjectives into verbs by adding these endings: -ate, -en, -ify, -ise.
e.g. fertile + ise = fertilise

wide _____   pure _____   special _____

beauty _____   fabric _____

THE PAST TENSES

If you want to describe something that happened earlier today, or yesterday, or a long time ago, you need to use one of the past tenses. Use a past tense if something is now finished, over and done with.

I **shouted** at Zelda but she took no notice.
I **did shout** at Zelda, I admit, but I won't do it again.
I **have shouted** at Zelda all day and I have a headache now.
I **had shouted** at Zelda before I realised.
I **used to shout** at Zelda but I don't now.
I **was shouting** at Zelda when you arrived.

Yeah, that was a really good day.

Each past tense means something slightly different.

YOUR SHOUT

Use the past tense of <u>shout</u> that works best in these gaps.

1. I _____ at Zelda when the postman came but I stopped as soon as I saw him.

2. I _____ at Zelda when I was much younger but I don't now.

3. I _____ at Zelda when I saw the mess she had made.

4. I _____ at Zelda only once in my life.

Usually you add -ed and -ing to a verb to help form the past tenses, but some can be very peculiar.

Look at these:

to swim	I **swam** in the pool.
	I **was swimming** in the pool.
	I **have swum** in the pool.
to begin	I **began** my homework.
	I **was beginning** my homework.
	I **have begun** my homework.
to do	I **did** my homework.
	I **was doing** my homework.
	I **have done** my homework.

Your dictionary will always help you with verbs that don't follow the usual pattern. Look up what is called the infinitive (to _____). The infinitives of the examples above are given on the left: to swim, to begin, to do.

RIGHT OR WRONG

Put a cross beside Steven's mistakes.
Tick any of the tenses he's got right.

1. Colin seen it.
2. I done it.
3. Zelda catched it.
4. We have selled it.
5. You taked it.

DO IT YOURSELF

Fill the gaps with the right part of the verb. (The infinitive is in brackets at the end.)

1. The baby has _____ up. (to wake)
2. Nobody _____ to me yesterday. (to speak)
3. The water pipes have _____ . (to freeze)
4. We all _____ to understand but we couldn't. (to try)
5. I _____ you had gone home. (to think)

THE FUTURE TENSES

Anything happening in a minute, or later today, or tomorrow, or after that will be in one of the future tenses.

Will you avoid shouting, this time, please?

There are several of them and there are slight differences in meaning.

I **shall ask** Zelda.
I **will ask** Zelda.

I **shall be asking** Zelda.
I **will be asking** Zelda.

I **am going to ask** Zelda.
I **am about to ask** Zelda.

Look at the last two examples. In both examples, I clearly plan to ask Zelda something but I'm closer to actually doing it in the second sentence.

<u>I am about to ask Zelda.</u> (= very soon now!)

Look at the middle two examples. In both sentences, Zelda is clearly going to be asked something in the future but in the second sentence there is more determination!

<u>I shall be asking Zelda.</u> (when I get a chance)
<u>I will be asking Zelda.</u> (whatever happens)

Similarly, with the first two examples. The first sentence suggests that Zelda will be asked in the normal course of events. The second sentence means that I fully intend to ask Zelda whatever it is that's on my mind!

Go on then. I'm listening!

Will it be OK if I do some more shouting?

AAAAAAAAARRRRRGGGGHHHH.

Notice how you can switch from simple future tense to a future tense full of determination and will-power.

Look carefully at **shall** and **will**.

SIMPLE FUTURE

Singular	Plural
I **shall** ask	we **shall** ask
you **will** ask	you **will** ask
he/she/it **will** ask	they **will** ask

FUTURE WITH DETERMINATION ADDED

Singular	Plural
I **will** ask	we **will** ask
you **shall** ask	you **shall** ask
he/she/it **shall** ask	they **shall** ask

> I WILL dance with you!

> I **will** die first!

> You SHALL go to the teashop for a light snack!

> I was sort of hoping for a ball, really.

Most people don't bother about the subtle difference in meaning between *shall* and *will* and possibly in time we shall all forget about it. That is how language develops. At the moment, however, the difference exists and it's worth taking care over.

And now an example of the tenses you've seen, in exciting action.

TROUSERS/TROUSERS/TROUSERS/TROUSERS/TROUSERS/TROUSE

YOUR CUT OUT 'N' KEEP TROUSER SOUVENIR.
THE AMAZING MR TROUSERS USES ALL THE TENSES IN ONE GO.

Is it a bird? Is it a plane? No... it's Mr Trousers...
Right here goes then... everybody ready? Right... "I used to wear short trousers, but in 1970 my legs got hairy, so until 1995 I wore long, baggy trousers. Now I wear long non-baggy trousers. One day, I shall wear no trousers at all. That'll make people take notice."
Cheer now! Accept no substitute.

Mr Trousers – original and best.

AUXILIARY VERBS

Otherwise known as HELPING verbs.

Verbs that help other verbs to make tenses are called auxiliary (or helping) verbs.

The most common auxiliary verbs are:

to be   **to have**   **to do**

I **did** enjoy your book.
I **have** devoured every page.
I **have been** chewing them.

My slide show of interesting milk bottle tops **will be** showing tonight. I **am** hoping you will come.

I'm sorry, I **will be** washing my hair.

Zelda **had been** dirtying it all day so that she **would** have an excuse.

Underline the auxiliary verbs in these sentences and put a box around the main verbs.

1. You do look nice.
2. Cinderella, you shall go to the ball.
3. I have forgotten your name.
4. My father was snoring very loudly.
5. He is learning French.

Add suitable auxiliary verbs in the spaces.

6. They _____ collecting firewood.
7. My neighbour _____ won £10,000.
8. Everybody _____ cheering very loudly at yesterday's match.
9. We _____ hear the results tomorrow.
10. I _____ not know the answer.

MORE AUXILIARY VERBS

might   must   could   would   should

These auxiliary verbs cause no trouble used like this:

> I **might** <u>tell</u>.
> I **must** <u>tell</u>.
> I **could** <u>tell</u>.
> I **would** <u>tell</u>.
> I **should** <u>tell</u>.

I **William Tell**.

But some people CAN'T HANDLE them in constructions like these:

I **might** of <u>told</u>. ✘	I **might** have <u>told</u>. ✔
I **must** of <u>told</u>. ✘	I **must** have <u>told</u>. ✔
I **could** of <u>told</u>. ✘	I **could** have <u>told</u>. ✔
I **would** of <u>told</u>. ✘	I **would** have <u>told</u>. ✔
I **should** of <u>told</u>. ✘	I **should** have <u>told</u>. ✔

If you want to shorten these constructions you can do it like this:

> I might've told.
> I must've told.
> I could've told.
> I would've told.
> I should've told.

But don't make the SILLY mistake of thinking that **must've** is written **must of**!!

Who would of thought it!

You could've — should've — used **would've**.

CONTRACTIONS

Otherwise known as shortened forms!

While we're talking about contractions like could've, let's revise a few more.

There are TWO in that last sentence!

I mean you're ... it's ... isn't it? ooh, He'd...
I'm er not sure about.. I'll... I'll...

Here are just a few:

I'll = I will	I'll phone you tomorrow.
I'll = I shall	I'll be ten years old tomorrow.
you've = you have	You've got very big eyes.
he'd = he had	He'd lost all his money.
he'd = he would	He'd have preferred to go to Spain.
we're = we are	We're sorry about that.
it's = it is	It's not fair.
it's = it has	It's been a lovely day.
can't = cannot	I can't hear you.
isn't = is not	It isn't fair.

NORMAL SIZE

Here's a brain.   **It's contracted.**   **It's tiny.**

Isn't that Steven's?

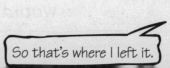

So that's where I left it.

WIN A TROPHY NOW!*

Put apostrophes where they're needed.
Some sentences DON'T need any!

1. If I have any more to eat Ill feel ill.
2. Its quite true that the cat chases its tail every evening.
3. I cant believe thats true.
4. Were sorry we werent there.
5. My chewing gum has lost its flavour.
6. Didnt you know that theyd moved?
7. Where were you yesterday?
8. Youre always moaning about your teachers.
9. I mustve told you who they are.
10. Your rabbit has broken its hutch.

If you get 9/10 or more, award yourself this:

THE APOS TROPHY

I am not stupid

* *This time it is true – hooray!*

THE INFINITIVE

We've talked about infinitives already. They're the basic form of the verb, usually beginning with to.

To Infinitive, And Beyond!

Here are some examples:

I tried **to ride** a camel in Egypt.
I hope **to go** to university.
They let me help them **(to) paint** the house.

When people talk about SPLIT INFINITIVES, they mean a word has been put in the middle of an infinitive.

My father started **to** noisily **snore**.
He decided **to** never **wash** again.

Usually there's no point in splitting an infinitive because the sentence would sound better if you didn't.

My father started to snore noisily. ✔
He decided never to wash again. ✔

BUT if you think your sentence would sound better IF YOU DID SPLIT the infinitive, then go ahead. It's NOT a crime. You're free to do it.

Are you advising them to *deliberately on certain occasions when they feel like it* split their infinitives? MONSTROUS!

Monstrous? Even I can tell he's split his infinitive all right!

THE SPLIT INFINITIVE SPECIAL EDITION FOR PEOPLE WITH TIME TO SLOWLY PASS

One of the most famous split infinitives of all time, including the future, is of course featured at the beginning of *Star Trek*.

To baldly go where no man has gone before.

Star Trek shows the way ahead. Not that we're all about to start wearing those tight-fitting sweatshirts and black trousers, but the split infinitive is becoming more and more acceptable.

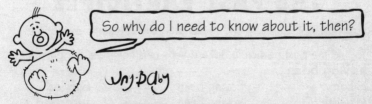

So why do I need to know about it, then?

Well, you should be aware that sometimes it sounds better not to split the infinitive, like in the examples opposite.

Perhaps more importantly, however, you can feel a little smug every time someone splits an infinitive badly.

THE PRESENT PARTICIPLE

PRESENT PARTICIPLE

Just what I was hoping to get —
a present participle.

PAST PARTICIPLE

So much better than
the past participle.

Present participles always end in **-ing**. They do TWO jobs:

1) They help to form tenses.
    Colin is **mowing** the lawn today.
    Colin was **mowing** the lawn yesterday.
    Colin will be **mowing** the lawn tomorrow.
2) They describe nouns and pronouns.
    <u>Colin</u> hurt his toe, **mowing** the lawn.
    <u>She</u> sat in the chair, **trembling** all over.

THE PAST PARTICIPLE

Past participles usually end in -ed but there are some exceptions.

To find the past participle, take a verb and complete the phrase:
having been . . .

to carry	having been	⟶	**carried**
to watch	having been	⟶	**watched**
to finish	having been	⟶	**finished**
to choose	having been	⟶	**chosen**
to buy	having been	⟶	**bought**
to see	having been	⟶	**seen**

Past participles can do TWO jobs too.

1) They help form tenses.
   The present was **chosen** with great care.
   Colin has **mown** the lawn.
2) They describe nouns and pronouns.
   Exhausted by his efforts, <u>Colin</u> rested.
   Watched by thousands, <u>he</u> crossed the line.

Be careful when you're using participles to describe nouns and pronouns. If you're not careful, they can describe the wrong ones.

Why is this sentence ridiculous?

MOWING THE LAWN, A STONE HIT COLIN ON THE NOSE.

It's ridiculous because it sounds as if it was THE STONE that was MOWING the lawn.

As we happen to know that it was Colin, we could rewrite the sentence in two ways to make it clear:

Mowing the lawn, Colin was hit on the nose by a stone.
While he was mowing the lawn, Colin was hit on the nose by a stone.

Always make sure that the participle relates to the right noun or to the right pronoun. Be on the look-out for any possible misunderstandings.

SPANNERS AT THE READY; IT'S REPAIR TIME

Can you rewrite these misleading sentences?

1. Walking round the corner,
   my cottage is on the left.

_____

2. Skipping happily across the road,
   a bicycle nearly knocked her over.

_____

3. Well known for ill-health and muggings,
   Mary Poppins lived in the London of the 1890s.

_____

COLIN'S CHALKBOARD CONCLUSIONS

VERBS

1. Verbs are doing and being words.
2. Auxiliary verbs help to make tenses.
3. Dictionaries help with irregular spellings.
4. There are no such constructions as:
   might of – must of – could of –
   would of – should of
   might have ✓ might've ✓.
5. Contractions need apostrophes.
6. Make sure participles describe the right
   noun or pronoun.

COLIN'S MISLEADING ADVICE NO. 14.

Parti-ciples are like disciples – except
they go to more parties. Because they
always bring a present, "present"
participles go to lots. "Past" parti-ciples
tend to go on about how they used to be
better, whereas Disco-ciples only go to...

ADVERBS

Adverbs mostly describe verbs. They add important information.
They tell us HOW, WHEN and WHERE things are done.

ADVERBS OF MANNER TELL US HOW SOMETHING IS DONE.

Colin droned on **endlessly**. My mother smiled **gently**.
Steven tries **hard**.

ADVERBS OF TIME TELL US WHEN SOMETHING IS DONE.

The doctor came **immediately**.   We all laughed **afterwards**.
I will always be **grateful**.

ADVERBS OF PLACE TELL US WHERE SOMETHING IS DONE.

I left the money **there**. We looked **everywhere**. Gather **round**.

ADVERBS OF DEGREE are a little different because they describe
other adverbs and adjectives.

My parents were **very** angry.
They were **extremely** cross.
They shouted **really** loudly.

"THE ADVERB FAMILY GOES COMPLETELY MAD"

THRILL as the family fights for its right to describe verbs –
accurately, repeatedly, fairly and often!
GASP as they swing into action, here, now, above you,
behind you, and everywhere!
CRY as they are used too frequently, badly, painfully, inappropriately.
SAY "THIS IS QUITE A LAUGH THEN" as the family runs
about idiotically, clumsily, and hilariously awkwardly!
STOP – suddenly.

ADVERBS

In order to liven up these exercises, we're going to do them whilst doing a line dance, OK? Everybody ready?
Take your partner by the hand and
Add an adverb where you stand.

1. The twins whispered _____ .

2. We made our beds _____ .

3. I ate the apple pie _____ .

4. We are _____ sorry for what we did.

5. Zelda tied the parcel _____ .

Bend over now y'all by the knees.
Make an adverb, er... if you please.
Careful y'all with the spelling
Otherwise, there's no telling (what will happen)

6. safe _____

7. careful _____

8. merry _____

9. sincere _____

10. real _____

Chicken in a basket, pickin' up sticks
See if you know the opposites (to these words).

11. seldom _____

12. most _____

13. quickly _____

14. always _____

15. loosely _____

Swing your elders, swing your betters
See if you can tell the missing letters
Listen now and pay good heed,
Use a dictionary if you need.

16. Mona Lisa is smiling enig __ __ __ __ cally.

17. Steven is smiling stu __ idly.

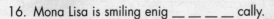

Dosey-do and eat the cake.
Can you pick out each mistake?
If you can, now put it right
Or else with me you'll have to fight.

18. I am learning to type proper.

19. Everyone is behaving really strange.

20. Zelda plays the flute beautiful.

21. He spoke rather fierce.

Now it's time to stop our prancing
And time for me to give up line dancing.
I really want to be a lumberjack.

SAY WHAT YOU MEAN

Be very careful when you use the adverbs HARDLY and SCARCELY.

If you use NOT in the same sentence, you could end up saying the very opposite of what you mean.

For example:

Colin's <u>not</u> wearing <u>hardly</u> any clothes.   *means*
Colin's wearing a lot of clothes.

If you mean to describe this awful sight . . .

then you should say:

Colin is wearing **hardly** any clothes.

BE VERY CAREFUL AGAIN

Take care when you use the word ONLY. It really does matter where you put it in a sentence. It will describe the nearest word.

Only <u>Zelda</u> can buy sweets on Fridays.
(= nobody else)

Zelda can buy **only** <u>sweets</u> on Fridays.
(= nothing else)

Zelda can buy sweets **only** <u>on Fridays</u>.
(= at no other time)

COMPARISON OF ADVERBS

Steven dives **gracefully**.

Colin dives **more gracefully**.

Zelda dives **most gracefully**.

Add **-er** and **-est** to short adverbs to make comparisons.

Steven works **hard**. (positive)
Colin works **harder**. (comparative)
Zelda works the **hardest**. (superlative)

Use **more** and **most** with other adverbs.

calmly	more calmly	most calmly
kindly	more kindly	most kindly
carelessly	more carelessly	most carelessly
energetically	more energetically	most energetically

Use **less** and **least** to go in the other direction.

energetically	less energetically	least energetically

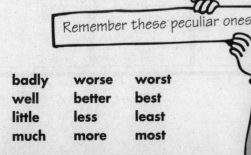

Remember these peculiar ones.

badly	**worse**	**worst**
well	**better**	**best**
little	**less**	**least**
much	**more**	**most**

73

Adjectives and adverbs together: The Hardest Test Known Ever, Brought Exclusively To You.

Start at number 1. See if you can say the answer out loud. If, when you move on to the square mentioned, you discover you got it right, answer the next question, and so on. When you get one wrong, go back to the start.

1 What is the comparative of the adverb "hard"? Go forward to 5.	**2** *Most softly.* What's the comparative? Go to 13.	**3** *Adverb – comparative of late.* What's the superlative of "many"? Go to 9.	**4** *Most tunefully.* What's the superlative of "near"? Go to 8.
8 *Nearest.* What part of speech is "later"? Go to 3.	**7** *Less.* What's the superlative of "softly"? Go to 2.	**6** *Adverb – superlative.* What's the superlative of "good"? Go to 10.	**5** *Harder.* What's the superlative of the adjective "easy"? Go to 12.
9 *Most.* What's the superlative of "badly"? Go forward to 14.	**10** *Best.* What's the superlative of "tunefully"? Go to 4.	**11** *Best.* What part of speech is "most clumsily"? Go to 6.	**12** *Easiest.* What's the comparative of the adverb "quietly"? Go to 15.
16 FINISHED! Tremendously well done. Most tremendously well done, in fact.	**15** *More quietly.* What's the superlative of "well"? Go to 11.	**14** *Worst.* What's the comparative of "little"? Go to 7.	**13** *More softly.* Go to 16.

COLIN'S CHALKBOARD CONCLUSIONS

ADVERBS

1. Adverbs describe verbs and other adverbs.

2. **Scarcely** and **hardly** are negatives.

3. Be careful to put **only** in front of the right word.

4. In comparisons, we use **-er** and **-est** with short adverbs; **more** and **most** with the others.

When you've 'ad enough of verbs by themselves, just 'add an adverb!

His attempts at humour are quickly, sadly, tragically getting worse.

JUST MESSING ABOUT

Some slang expressions have entered the language from the East End of London from Cockney rhyming slang.

You'll know some of them:

plates of <u>meat</u>	feet
trouble and <u>strife</u>	wife
apples and <u>pears</u>	stairs

Some expressions are not so straightforward because the rhyming word is left out!

use your loaf   (loaf of <u>bread</u>)   use your head

me ol' China   (china <u>plate</u>)   mate

Here are some more Cockney rhyming slang phrases.

chew the <u>fat</u>	have a chat
not a dickey-<u>bird</u>	not a word
mince <u>pies</u>	eyes
daisy <u>roots</u>	boots
Cain & <u>Abel</u>	table
skin and <u>blister</u>	sister
God <u>forbids</u>	kids
Hampstead <u>Heath</u>	teeth
North & <u>South</u>	mouth
dog and <u>bone</u>	phone
raspberry <u>(tart)</u>	heart
Oliver <u>(Twist)</u>	fist
titfer (tit for <u>tat</u>)	hat
bread (and <u>honey</u>)	money
porkies (pork <u>pies</u>)	lies

> After I hurt me plates, I was talking to my skin and blister on the dog and bone with me raspberry in my daisies, straight up.

> What!?

PREPOSITIONS

Prepositions are little words like

on **by** **from** **for** **with** **to** **of** **in** **at**

You'll see from these examples the important job they do in sentences. They show connections.

My cat is hiding **under** the bed.

Your coat is **on** the floor.

This poem is **by** Roald Dahl.

Here is a message **from** the Queen.

Give that **to** me.

SHIP IN A BOTTLE

PREPOSITIONS

Notice that in the last example, the pronoun form is **me** not I.

Use me, you, him, her, us, them after prepositions.

This <u>invitation</u> is **for** <u>you</u>.
This <u>invitation</u> is **for** <u>me</u>.
This <u>invitation</u> is **for** <u>you and me</u>.
This <u>invitation</u> is **for** <u>us</u>.

This chocolate is for us.   **This chocolate is for me.**

SPOT THE DIFFERENCE

What's the difference in meaning in each pair?

1. drop in

   drop out

2. laugh at

   laugh off

3. give away

   give up

DON'T BE PREPOSTEROUS

PREPOSTEROUS REX (EXTINCT)

Choose the right preposition.

Your dictionary will help you.

1. They're always complaining _____ us.

2. We're hoping _____ good results.

3. I prefer chocolate _____ sweets.

4. She agrees _____ everything you say.

5. My uncle has given _____ smoking.

CAN YOU END A SENTENCE WITH A PREPOSITION?

Some people say that you never should. Others say that it all depends on whether the sentence sounds better with a preposition at the end or somewhere else.

Generally speaking, most sentences sound better if they don't end with a preposition. Compare these two questions:

Can you use a preposition to end a sentence **with**?
Can you end a sentence **with** a preposition?

However, there are other cases where the sentence sounds really peculiar if you try to avoid having the preposition at the end:

What are you waiting **for**?
For what are you waiting?

Make up your own mind. Try the sentence both ways and then decide.

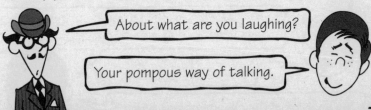

About what are you laughing?

Your pompous way of talking.

COLIN'S CHALKBOARD CONCLUSIONS

PREPOSITIONS

1. Prepositions are little words that connect.

2. Use the right preposition. Your dictionary will help you.

3. End a sentence with a preposition if it sounds better that way.

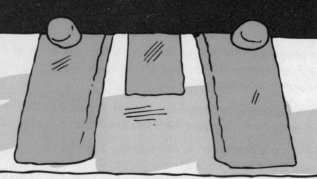

So this man, right, comes up to me and says, right, that he can prove that his favourite parts of speech are the little fleshy bits of the fruit with a stone in it, away from the furry skin. So I say to him... "That's a ridiculous preposition!" Get it? A ridiculous — not proposition, but "preposition"!

Does it occur to you he might have been talking about "parts of peach"?

Ah, no.

Nurse! Nurse! Colin's out of bed again.

CONJUNCTIONS AND INTERJECTIONS

Conjunctions JOIN.

and ANDCUFFS.

COORDINATING CONJUNCTIONS

and　　but　　or

These join two of the same kind and keep them equally important.

> fish **and** chips
> slowly **but** surely
> sink **or** swim

Make sure you always choose the one you need. They each have a different meaning and some people don't realise that.

and　　but　　or

Use each just once in the right place.

1. He is tired _____ he won't stop.

2. Do you like maths _____ English best?

3. Holidays are fun _____ I always look forward to them.

Now use them all in one sentence:

> I know the things I want to do to Colin _____ I have the right machinery, _____ all are either illegal _____ not painful enough.

81

CORRELATIVE CONJUNCTIONS

not only . . . but also
both . . . and
either . . . or
neither . . . nor

He's **not only** handsome **but also** intelligent.
His mother was **both** amazed **and** delighted.
You are **either** mad **or** thinking of someone else.
I have **neither** forgotten **nor** forgiven the time he sat gnawing a
bone for an hour. When he stood up his leg fell off.

> You do have to be **both**
> very sensible **and** very careful!

It's true you have to be careful where you put
each half of the pair to keep the sentence balanced.

My mother either told me to tidy my
room or to take the dog for a walk. ✗

My mother told me   1) to tidy my room
                 2) to take the dog for a walk

My mother told me **either** to tidy
my room **or** to take the dog for a walk. ✓

PUT THIS SENTENCE RIGHT

Steven not only is lazy but also greedy.

> Steven is fab?

No. I mean put it right grammatically.

SUBORDINATING CONJUNCTIONS

These join by making one statement follow on from another in a dependent way.

WHY?

She did well   **because** she worked hard.

WHEN?

Zelda will contact you   **when** the spare part comes.

HOW?

He looked   **as though** he'd seen a ghost.

WHY?

I gave her a lift   **because** she was late.

Here are some subordinating conjunctions:

after	**if***	**until**
although	**in order that**	**when**
as	**since**	**whenever**
as if	**so . . . that**	**where**
as though	**so that**	**wherever**
because	**that**	**whether***
before	**though**	**while**
for	**unless**	**whilst**

*__if__ and **whether** are alternatives.

You must finish the sentence... and make it funny!

1. Wait here until _____ .
2. He cleared his throat before _____ .
3. I'll buy the bicycle if _____ .
4. Sandra enjoyed the book because _____ .
5. My father doubled my pocket money, although _____ .

Pick a conjunction – any conjunction.

6. Sally can dance _____ she's playing the violin.
7. I tripped over the mat _____ I came in.
8. He doesn't know _____ he'll be in London.
9. We like Zelda _____ she's very kind.
10. My dog follows me _____ I go.

INTERJECTIONS

When you hurt your toe and say "**Ouch!**", you are using an interjection.

When you jump in the air and say "**Yippee!**", you are using an interjection.

Interjections are short exclamations that express feelings.

Here are some that express pain, delight, joy, relief, shock, horror, disgust and fear.

CAPTAIN INTERJECTION

DOCTOR INJECTION

Ow! Ouch! Yippee! Hooray! Gosh! Wow! Phew! Ah! Oh! Oh dear! Aaargh! Bah! Help! Ugh! Boo! Oops! Pshaw!

Interjections can be written as separate sentences of their own or they can be written as separate parts at the beginning of longer sentences.

OI! YOU! NOW!

Write a sentence that fits the interjection.

1. Ouch!

2. Yippee!

3. Gosh!

4. Ugh!

5. Wow!

How about "Yippee! I'm a hippy!"?

COLIN'S CHALKBOARD CONCLUSIONS

CONJUNCTIONS AND INTERJECTIONS

1. Conjunctions join.

2. Use the right conjunction.

3. Correlative conjunctions are used in pairs. Put each half of the pair in the right place.

4. Interjections are short exclamations.

5. Interjections can be used on their own or at the beginning of sentences.

Not only...
Ow!
but also...
Ugh!
and...
OOO!
and...
Umph!
not just...
Ouch!
and...
Help!
but also...

JUST MESSING ABOUT

All the abbreviations below are abbreviations of Latin words.
Do you know the Latin words they stand for?

A.D.	anno domini	in the year of the Lord
a.m.	ante meridiem	before noon
cf.	confer	compare
C.V.	curriculum vitae	summary of career and life
D.V.	Deo volente	if God is willing
e.g.	exempli gratia	for example
etc.	et cetera	and the rest
i.e.	id est	that is
l.i.d.b	latinus ista deadus boringus	Latin is dead boring (not a real one)
N.B.	nota bene	note carefully
p.m.	post meridiem	after noon
P.S.	post scriptum	after the writing
R.I.P.	requiescat in pace	may he/she rest in peace
Q.E.D.	quid erat demonstrandum	which was to be shown or proved
v.	versus	against
viz	videlicit	namely

Is R.S.V.P. Latin?

No, it's from the French:
Répondez s'il vous plaît.
It means: please reply.

I don't think I'll bother!

Do you ever get muddled up when you use **e.g.** and **i.e.**?
Use **e.g.** when you are going to give an example.
Citrus fruits, **e.g.** lemons and oranges, are rich in Vitamin C.
Use **i.e.** when you are going to give an explanation or a
definition. All external examination candidates, **i.e.** those
taking GCSE and A-level examinations, should stay behind
after Assembly.

SENTENCES

Of all the parts of speech that we have studied, which is the one vital one in a sentence?

Well, yes. It's ONE of those but *WHICH ONE?*

Let's put the question another way.
Look at the three sentences below.
One is a statement, one is a question and one is a command.
What is the ONE part of speech they have in common?

> We ate three doughnuts each.
> Are you interested?
> Look!

Each sentence has a . . .

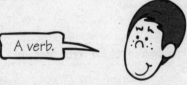

A verb.

Each sentence has a verb and it's a very special kind of verb.

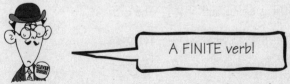

A FINITE verb!

Well done! Each sentence has a finite verb and you haven't learnt about these yet.

Turn to the next page and you'll learn about FINITE VERBS.

FINITE VERBS

Finite verbs have subjects.

Don't panic! Come back. We'll explain.

In the sentences below, we've put the subjects in boxes and underlined the verbs.

| Steven | is laughing.

| The grass | is being cut.

| Lollipops | make you sticky.

| We | have lost our way.

Put WHO or WHAT in front of the verbs and you'll find the subjects.

WHO is laughing?   Steven

WHAT is being cut?   The grass

WHAT make you sticky?   Lollipops

WHO have lost the way?   We

All the sentences above are statements. Commands and questions have subjects too but they're not quite so easy to find. We'll look at commands first.

LOOK OUT!

WHO should look out? (It doesn't say but you jolly well know who's meant to look out if someone shouts at you!) YOU.

<u>Come</u> here!   You <u>come</u> here!

<u>Shut</u> up!   You <u>shut</u> up!

<u>Go</u> to bed!   You <u>go</u> to bed!

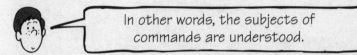

In other words, the subjects of commands are understood.

Yes. You can call them UNDERSTOOD, or IMPLIED, or TAKEN FOR GRANTED or LEFT OUT FOR THE SAKE OF BREVITY. But the verbs in commands are finite verbs. They could have their subjects there if they wanted.

Now let's look at questions. The word order in questions is a bit complicated as the subjects can come later than in statements.

<u>Is</u> **Steven** <u>laughing</u>?
<u>Is</u> **the grass** <u>being cut</u>?
<u>Do</u> **lollipops** <u>make</u> you sticky?
<u>Have</u> **we** <u>lost</u> our way?

OK?

So to sum up:

EVERY SENTENCE (WHETHER A COMMAND, A QUESTION, OR A STATEMENT) HAS TO HAVE A FINITE VERB.

Yes, it does.

That's right.

He's got it, you know.

He has, yes.

SENTENCES

Now take a deep breath because we are going to spend half a page talking about non-finite verbs.

They sound complicated but they're not!

NON-FINITE VERBS

the infinitive
the present participle
the past participle

Do you remember these from the section on verbs?

to choose	infinitive
choosing	present participle
chosen	past participle

They're not finite verbs because they can't have subjects and so they can't be sentences on their own. Even if you wrote them out neatly with a capital letter at the beginning and a full stop at the end, they wouldn't be sentences.

They wouldn't be sentences because EVERY SENTENCE NEEDS A FINITE VERB and the infinitive, the present participle and the past participle are NOT finite verbs. They are only parts of verbs.

EVERY SENTENCE NEEDS A FINITE VERB.

He's still right.

He's got it, that boy.

Sure is.

Sure has.

FIND THE SENTENCES

There are three sentences hidden here.
Write them properly punctuated in the spaces at the end.

1. laughing all the way to the bank.
2. he was very cross
3. to cook a really delicious meal
4. chosen as partners
5. my mother gave me 50p
6. burnt to a cinder
7. coming round the corner without looking.
8. you must be joking
9. mowing the lawn before breakfast
10. reduced for a second time

_____

_____

_____

Elementary, my dear Watson.

A lemon entry?

JUST MESSING ABOUT TIME FOR WOULD-BE GENIUSES

Questions are written with a question mark at the end. Agreed?

"How are you?" he asked.
"Would you like an ice-cream?" she enquired.

If you make these questions into reported statements, you won't need question marks or speech marks.

He asked me how I was.
She asked if I would like an ice-cream.

Similarly, shouted commands are written with an exclamation mark at the end.

"Stand still boy!" ordered the angry teacher.
"Go to bed!" said my mother firmly.

If you make these commands into reported statements, you won't need exclamation marks or speech marks.

The angry teacher ordered the boy to stand still.
My mother told me firmly to go to bed.

The policeman ordered the police to stop. The thief asked the policeman why he didn't stop instead.

A QUESTIONABLE COMMAND PERFORMANCE

Change these commands and questions into statements

1. "Blow your nose!" ordered my father.

   My father ordered me _____ .

2. "Get up!" my mother said to my sister.

   My mother told my sister_____ .

3. "Are you feeling better?" asked my teacher.

   My teacher asked me_____ .

4. "How much are the tomatoes?" the old lady asked the shopkeeper.

   The old lady asked the shop keeper_____.

5. "Will you tie my shoelaces?" my little brother asked.

   My little brother asked me _____ .

The aggressively forgetful vicar checked with the parents whether their child's name was Toby.

IMPROVING YOUR SENTENCES

If you're happy with your written style, then this section is not so important for you – although *everybody* can improve.

If, on the other hand, you're not happy when you read through your work, if you know you've written in short jerky sentences but don't know what you can do about them, then you should find this section useful.

You'll find that you can experiment in all sorts of ways with combining short sentences into longer more complex ones. Remember, of course, that, used sparingly, short sentences can often be very effective. You really want a careful mixture of sentences of different lengths.

Be critical of your work. Don't be content with the first draft if you feel it can be improved. Be prepared to write several drafts of an important piece of work until it reads as well as you can make it.

Let's assume, for instance, that you've written this paragraph and are not happy with it:

> We all decided to go to Exmouth on Sunday. It was very hot. We were determined to swim. We all stayed in the water for a long time. We had each brought a packed lunch. We shared everything. We had a game of cricket on the sands. We all enjoyed that. It got rather cold in the middle of the afternoon. We decided to go home early. We'd had a really good time.

But that makes perfect sense... Why can't I be happy with that?

Well...

Some people are bossy. They say keep them short. Fine. You can read them easily. That's good. For a bit. But not all the time. Eh? It starts getting irritating. Doesn't it? Like someone jabbing you. Going, "Hm?", "Hm?", "Hm?"...

MR. JERKY

Having said that, don't imagine for one moment that all your sentences should be long because that would be wrong for the simple reason that this sort of sentence eventually gets harder and harder to follow, quite apart from being

terribly dull.

So you might want to vary the length. That's why you need to know ways of joining.

MR. VARIETY

Coordinating conjunctions: <u>and</u>, <u>but</u>, <u>or</u>

You don't want to rely solely on coordinating conjunctions. (You could end up with an awful rambling paragraph: we all decided to go to Exmouth on Sunday and it was very hot and we were . . .) However, one or two could certainly help our disjointed paragraph.

Perhaps:

> It was very hot and we were determined to swim.

or:

> We were determined to swim and we all stayed in the water for some time.

NOW you know why you shouldn't start a sentence with AND or BUT or OR. They are words for *joining* sentences and so will be somewhere in the middle of a sentence, not at the beginning.

SUBORDINATING CONJUNCTIONS

after	**although**	**as**	**as if**	**as though**	**because**
before	**for**	**if**	**in order that**	**since**	**so . . . that**
so that	**that**	**though**	**unless**	**until**	**when**
whenever	**where**	**wherever**	**while**	**whilst**	

Here are just a few of the possible combinations:

Sunday was **so** hot **that** we all decided to go to Exmouth.

As it got rather cold in the middle of the afternoon, we decided to go home early.

Although we went home early **because** it got cold in the middle of the afternoon, we'd had a really good time.

USING WHO, WHOM, WHOSE, WHICH, THAT

Use **who** and **whom** for people.

Use **which** and **that** for things.

Whose can refer to both people and things.

Zelda is the person **who** does all the work around here.

She is the person **whom** I admire most.

Either: We had each brought a packed lunch **which** we shared.

or: We had each brought a packed lunch **that** we shared.

Either: We had a game of cricket on the sands **which** we all enjoyed.

or: We had a game of cricket on the sands **that** we all enjoyed.

USING PARTICIPLES

Determined to swim, we all stayed in the water for a long time.

Having each **brought** a packed lunch, we shared everything.

After **sharing** the packed lunches each of us had brought, we had a game of cricket on the sands.

BEING MORE CONCISE

You may find that you can use just a few words to replace a whole sentence.

> We had a game of cricket on the sands. We all enjoyed that.
>
> = We all had an enjoyable game of cricket on the sands.
>
> We had each brought a packed lunch. We shared everything.
>
> = We shared our packed lunches.

No two people would rewrite the paragraph in exactly the same way. There are so many possibilities that no two people would choose exactly the same set in the same sequence.

Here is one possible second draft:

> Sunday was so hot that we all decided to go to Exmouth. We were determined to swim and stayed in the water for a long time. After sharing our packed lunches, we had an enjoyable game of cricket on the sands. Although we went home early because it got cold in the middle of the afternoon, we'd had a really good time.

You might want to work further on this, tinkering and polishing, of course. Drafting and redrafting is a very important part of the creative process.

GET IT TOGETHER

Use any method you like to combine each of these groups of short sentences into single sentences.

1. Matt tidied his bedroom. He washed up the breakfast things. He had forgotten to buy a present. It was Mother's Day.

    _____

    _____

2. I have flu. I have all the usual symptoms. I have a sore throat. I have a high temperature. I don't feel like eating anything. I have no energy.

    _____

    _____

    _____

3. Sarah was nervous. It was her first day at her new school. She knew nobody. It was a huge building. "I shall get lost," she thought. She had a different teacher for every lesson. It was confusing at first.

    _____

    _____

    _____

    _____

SENTENCE BOUNDARIES

No, Steven. Not that kind of boundary.

Always take care to show where one sentence ends and another begins.

This may sound very simple but you'd be AMAZED at how many people don't use end stops (full stops), or question marks, or exclamation marks at the ends of sentences. You don't want to be stupid like them, do you?

Is that why END STOPS are called END STOPS because they go at the END?

Yes, Steven, it is. What's more, ONLY end stops will do – you can't use commas instead. Commas can't do the special work of a full stop, a question mark, or an exclamation mark. Commas can't show where a sentence ends.

ROADSIDE CHECK

Circle the four places where full stops are needed instead of commas.

As a half-term treat, Steven, Colin and Zelda are going camping in the New Forest, fortunately they've been able to borrow a tent, a groundsheet and a camping-stove, they already have warm sleeping bags, all week, it seems, they have been making lists, buying last-minute items, and packing rucksacks, the weather forecast is not very good but they'll enjoy themselves whatever the weather, if I know them.

COLIN'S DIARY

Colin says that he'll put the end stops in when he gets home. Can you help by circling all the places where he needs a full stop, a question mark or an exclamation mark?

Friday 30 May

We managed to get the tent up Steven wasn't much help it's lucky that I know something about camping Zelda forgot to pack the mallet fortunately I thought of using a tin of baked beans to bang the tent pegs in with what would they do without me they've got no ideas of their own

Saturday 31 May

It rained all night luckily our sleeping bags are still dry it was Steven's turn to cook today we had a dreadful breakfast what will he be giving us tonight the New Forest ponies are very timid can you blame them Steven wanted to ride on one they ran away pretty fast

Sunday 1 June

The sun came out this morning it's been really hot we went for a long walk and we found some interesting-looking mushrooms we decided NOT to cook them we don't want to risk being poisoned Zelda's parents are coming to collect us at five o'clock it's been a good weekend but I've had to do most of the work I seem to be the only sensible one here I suppose I'm a natural leader

COLIN'S CHALKBOARD CONCLUSIONS

SENTENCES

1. Every sentence needs a subject and a verb.

2. Every sentence needs an end stop.

3. Try combining short, jerky sentences in different ways.

4. Always take time drafting and redrafting important pieces of written work.

Remember, sentences can be short and pithy like, "He who hesitates is lost".

Or long: "He who forgets to write down the directions and loses the map is in a number of serious difficulties, too".

But the most important advice is — DON'T BE LIKE COLIN.

Oi!

SOME MISTAKES PEOPLE MAKE

accept / except

We **accept** your invitation with great pleasure. (verb)
Everyone was there **except** Ann. (preposition)

They all wanted to accept Colin.   **They all wanted to,
                                                  except Colin.**

affect / effect

Winning the lottery will not **affect** my life. (verb)
The **effect** of the medicine was immediate. (noun)

allowed / aloud

Are we **allowed** to bring our pets? (verb)
Read your poem **aloud** to the class. (adverb)

Not allowed to speak aloud

are / our

Are you happy now? (verb)
They've been **our** friends for ages. (adjective)

as / has

Could you close the door **as** you leave? (conjunction)
Hugo **has** huge hands. (verb)

bought / brought

Have you **bought** all your Christmas presents yet? (verb – to buy)
We **brought** the plants to school in carrier bags. (verb – to bring)

**I bought you a present,
I haven't brought it.**

It brought me.

breath / breathe

I need a **breath** of fresh air. (noun)
Breathe deeply and fill those lungs. (verb)

buy / by

Where can I **buy** British bacon in Bradford? (verb)
This book is written **by** a friend of mine. (preposition)

does / dose

Mrs. Green **does** annoy me. (rhymes with fuzz) (verb)
Here's your **dose** of vitamins. (rhymes with gross) (preposition)

draw / drawer

You can **draw** cars beautifully. (verb)
The bottom **drawer** of the chest is jammed. (noun)

Quick on the drawer

hear / here

Can you **hear** me at the back? (verb)
I'm over **here** by the window. (adverb)

> I can hear you, but I'll change places with someone in here who can't.

Very Old Jokes of the World, no. 53

lay / lie (verbs)

to **lay** (the table)   to **lie** (down)   to (tell a) **lie**
to **lay** (an egg)

↓   ↓   ↓

She is **laying** the table.   He is **lying** down.   They are **lying**.
She **lays** the table.   He **lies** down.   They **lie**.
She has **laid** the table.   He has **lain** down.   They have **lied**.
She **laid** the table.   He **lay** down.   They **lied**.
She was **laying** the table.   He was **lying** down.   They were **lying**.

licence / license

You need a **licence**. (noun)
The village hall isn't **licensed** for a bar. (verb)

I'm waiter. A waiter.

Licensed to bill

lightening / lightning

They are **lightening** the load. (verb)
The **lightning** lit up the night sky. (noun)

like / as

You look **like** your father. (preposition)
As I told you, everything will be all right. (conjunction)
You look **as if** you've seen a ghost. (conjunction)

loose / lose

Shall I pull out that **loose** tooth? (adjective)
Don't **lose** your temper with me! (verb)

no / now / know

No, I won't come with you. (opposite of yes) (adverb)
Now I understand. (adverb)
Do you **know** when we break up? (verb)

of / off

She's the proud mother **of** ten children. (preposition)
Turn the light **off**. (adverb)

passed / past

Everyone has **passed** the exam. (verb)
She rushed **past** me. (preposition)

The ghost of Christmas Past   **The ghost of Christmas passed.**

practice / practise

An hour's **practice** every day is essential. (noun)
Practise the exercises every day. (verb)

SOME MISTAKES PEOPLE MAKE

principal / principle

My **principal** reason for taking the job is the money. (adjective)
Mrs Green is **Principal**. (= principal teacher)
I won't bet on **principle**. (noun)

I won't bet on Principal.

quiet / quite

You're so **quiet** that I thought you were asleep. (adjective)
I feel **quite** pleased at the result. (adverb)

stationary / stationery

Was the car **stationary** when you crashed into it? (adjective)
I usually give her **stationery** at Christmas. (noun)

to / too / two

Would you like **to** go **to** the cinema? (prepositions)
You've given me far **too** much **too**. (adverb)
I've lost **two** pencils today. (adjective)

One lost two games too.

One would've liked to have won one.

weather / whether

It all depends on the weather. (noun)
I don't know whether you agree. (conjunction)

who / whom

He is the man **who** sold me the bicycle. (pronoun)
(= He is the man. <u>He</u> sold me the bicycle.)
He is the man **whom** you described. (pronoun)
or He is the man you described.
(= He is the man. You described <u>him</u>. It is acceptable to leave out the word *whom* altogether in this sentence.)
Who sold you the bicycle? (Answer: <u>he</u> did) (pronoun)
Whom did you describe? (Answer: I described <u>him</u>) (pronoun)

Using *whom* may sound old-fashioned sometimes, but it does have a different meaning to *who* and you should take care to use the right word, especially when you are writing.

The Grammar Repair Kit M.O.T. (Master/Mistress of Things) Certificate

This Certificate is awarded to

_____

in recognition of his/her fantastic achievement. Not only can he/she now handle pronouns (like "he" and "she") but also nouns (like "achievement"), adjectives (like "fantastic", man) and verbs ("is", obviously) and will never need to be tense about tenses, apologetic about apostrophes or get conjunctivitis over conjunctions – a singular achievement for someone whose talents are now plural.

He/she need never again look stupid.
Well, grammatically speaking anyway. (Is there any other way?)

Signed

Zelda

Colin

Steven

Why-Baby

Clevertrousers

Stanley Savenergy

ANSWERS

(page numbers are in brackets)

NOUNS

FIND THE WORDS – WIN A TROPHY (8)

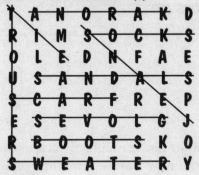

NAME THE BREED (9)

1. alsatian
2. poodle
3. sheepdog
4. bulldog
5. spaniel

HUNT THE PROPER NOUNS (13)

Manchester, Wales, Brian, Norway, Everest

GENERAL KNOWLEDGE QUIZ (13)

1. Roald Dahl
2. William
3. Stockholm
4. Thor
5. January, February, March, April etc etc. All of them. This is a trick question, which is why the Proper Little Devil was there. All the months have 28 days – some have even more!

COLLECTIVE STRENGTH TEST (14)

1. flock
2. fleet / convoy
3. galaxy / constellation
4. shoal
5. gang

ANSWERS

VERY ADVANCED GRAMMATICAL POINT (17)
1. is
2. was
3. is
4. were
5. was

MEMO TO TROOPS (17)
is, is, realises

ENDINGS (18)
1. friendship
2. nervousness
3. boyhood
4. kingdom
5. loyalty
6. excitement
7. justice
8. failure
9. cruelty
10. gentleness

TESTING, TESTING (19)
1. loneliness
2. misery
3. confidence
4. generosity
5. cowardice
6. laziness
7. pride
8. width
9. bravery
10. nobility
11. beauty

GENDER-AL KNOWLEDGE (21)
MASCULINE: nephew, ram, bull, grandfather
FEMININE: nun, heiress, daughter, queen
COMMON: judge, doctor, pet, teacher
NEUTER: chair, book, telephone, desk

STAND-INS (21)

1. head / head teacher / principal
2. priest / vicar / cleric / member of the clergy
3. supervisor / work leader / team leader
4. police officer / police constable
5. spokesperson / representative / leader

PECULIAR PLURALS (26)

The two words in the singular are mouse and man. Their plurals
are MICE and MEN.

EPONYMS (31)

1. nicotine
2. teddy bear
3. guillotine
4. biro
5. sandwich
6. JCB

PRONOUNS

CHOOSE THE RIGHT PRONOUN (34)

1. me
2. we
3. me
4. they
5. she

I OR ME (35)

1. I
2. me
3. me
4. I
5. me

ANSWERS

CHECK THAT YOU UNDERSTAND (36)
1. his   yours
2. theirs   mine

WORDS AND DERIVATIONS (40)

bungalow	–	(Hindi) Bengal thatched house
dandelion	–	(French) lion's tooth
dinghy	–	(Hindi) a small boat
ketchup	–	(Malay) fish sauce
khaki	–	(Urdu & Persian) dusty
patio	–	(Spanish) a courtyard
pyjamas	–	(Hindustani) leg clothing
robot	–	(Czech) compulsory labour
spaghetti	–	(Italian) little strings
spider	–	(Old English) a spinner
terminus	–	(Latin) end, limit
thug	–	(Hindi) robber, murderer
vermicelli	–	(Italian) little worms

ADJECTIVES

STAMP OUT THE EVIL INTRUDER (42)
1. bed
2. apple
3. across
4. car
5. myself

SPELLING QUIZ (45)
15   fifteen
40   forty
90   ninety
5th   fifth
8th   eighth
12th twelfth

SPOT TEST (47)
1. who's
2. whose
3. whose
4. who's
5. whose

SPOT CHECK (47)
1. its
2. its
3. it's
4. its
5. it's

AMERICANISMS (52)
1. biscuits   2. draughts   3. quilt
4. pedestrian crossing   5. pack   6. nappy   7. lift
8. autumn   9. tap   10. bumper
11. dustbin / rubbish bin   12. petrol   13. bonnet
14. flyover   15. baby's dummy   16. trousers
17. handbag   18. pavement   19. pushchair   20. boot

VERBS

ROADSIDE CHECK (55)
1. hate
2. punched
3. are
4. eats
5. bought
6. swallow

TEST YOUR UNDERSTANDING (55)
(possible answers)
1. Give me a kiss. (noun)
    Kiss your mother. (verb)
2. Do some work. (noun)
    Work harder. (verb)
3. Your help has been valuable. (noun)
    Help! (verb)
4. I had a dream last night. (noun)
    We dream every night. (verb)
5. We went for a long walk. (noun)
    Walk faster. (verb)

DICTIONARY WORK (55)
widen
purify
specialise
beautify
fabricate

YOUR SHOUT (56)
1. was shouting
2. used to shout
3. shouted
4. have shouted

RIGHT OR WRONG (57)
1. X
2. X
3. X
4. X
5. X (Well, it was Steven)

DO IT YOURSELF (57)
1. woken
2. spoke
3. frozen
4. tried
5. thought

AUXILIARY VERBS (60)
1. do look
2. shall go
3. have forgotten
4. was snoring
5. is learning
6. have been / had been
7. has / had
8. was
9. shall / will
10. do / did

WIN A TROPHY NOW! (63)
1.   . . . I'll feel
2.   It's quite true . . .
3.   can't . . . that's
4.   we're . . .weren't
5.   ✓
6.   Didn't . . . they'd
7.   ✓
8.   you're
9.   must've
10. ✓

SPANNERS AT THE READY (67)
1.   When you walk round the corner, my cottage is on the left.
2.   When she was skipping happily across the road, a bicycle nearly knocked her over.
3.   Mary Poppins lived in the London of the 1890s which was famous for ill-health and muggings.

ADVERBS

ADD AN ADVERB (70–71)
(Other answers are possible for 1-5.)
1. softly   2. neatly   3. quickly   4. truly   5. firmly
6. safely   7. carefully   8. merrily   9. sincerely
10. really   11. often   12. least   13. slowly
14. never   15. tightly   16. enigmatically   17. stupidly
18. properly   19. strangely   20. beautifully   21. fiercely

PREPOSITIONS

SPOT THE DIFFERENCE (78)
1.   drop in – visit unexpectedly, arrive casually
     drop out – give up, withdraw
2.   laugh at – jeer, sneer, ridicule
     laugh off – treat something (like an injury) as if it doesn't matter
3.   give away – give for no charge / betray
     give up – abandon, surrender, stop trying

CHOOSE THE RIGHT PREPOSITION (79)

1. about
2. for
3. to
4. with
5. up

CONJUNCTIONS AND INTERJECTIONS

AND, BUT, OR (81)

1. but
2. or
3. and

Zelda: I know the things I want to do to Colin and I have the right machinery, but all are either illegal or not painful enough.

PUT THAT SENTENCE RIGHT (82)

Steven is not only lazy but also greedy.

CHOOSE A CONJUNCTION (83)

6. as/while
7. as/before/after/when
8. when/if/whether
9. because/as/since/for
10. wherever

OI! YOU! NOW! (84)

1. (Express pain.)
2. (Express delight.)
3. (Express surprise.)
4. (Express disgust.)
5. (Express delight and surprise.)

SENTENCES

FIND THE SENTENCES (91)

2. He was very cross.
3. My mother gave me 50p.
8. You must be joking.

A QUESTIONABLE COMMAND PERFORMANCE (93)
1. My father ordered me to blow my nose.
2. My mother told my sister to get up.
3. My teacher asked me whether / if I was feeling better.
4. The old lady asked the shopkeeper how much the tomatoes were / the cost of the tomatoes / the price of the tomatoes.
5. My little brother asked me to tie his shoelaces / if I would tie his shoe laces / whether I would tie his shoelaces.

ROADSIDE CHECK (99)
As a half-term treat, Steven, Colin and Zelda are going camping in the New Forest ⊙ Fortunately they've been able to borrow a tent, a groundsheet and a campingstove ⊙ They already have warm sleeping bags ⊙ All week, it seems, they have been making lists, buying last-minute items, and packing rucksacks ⊙ The weather forecast is not very good but they'll enjoy themselves whatever the weather, if I know them.

COLIN'S DIARY (100)
(alternative punctuation in brackets)

Friday 30 May
We managed to get the tent up. (!) Steven wasn't much help. (!) It's lucky that I know something about camping. (!) Zelda forgot to pack the mallet. Fortunately I thought of using a tin of baked beans to bang the tent pegs in with. What would they do without me? They've got no ideas of their own. (!)

Saturday 31 May
It rained all night. (!) Luckily our sleeping bags are still dry. It was Steven's turn to cook today. We had a dreadful breakfast. (!) What will he be giving us tonight? The New Forest ponies are very timid. Can you blame them? Steven wanted to ride on one. (!) They ran away pretty fast!

Sunday 1 June
The sun came out this morning. It's been really hot. We went for a long walk and we found some interesting-looking mushrooms. We decided NOT to cook them. (!) We don't want to risk being poisoned. (!) Zelda's parents are coming to collect us at five o'clock. It's been a good weekend but I've had to do most of the work. I seem to be the only sensible one here. (!) I suppose I'm a natural leader. (!)

INDEX

ORDER FORM

0 340 74649 1	Grammar Repair Kit	£3.99	☐
0 340 64679 9	Maths Repair Kit	£3.99	☐
0 340 63618 1	Punctuation Repair Kit	£3.99	☐
0 340 77838 5	Science Repair Kit	£3.99	☐
0 340 66496 7	Spelling Repair Kit	£3.99	☐

Turn the page to find out how to order these books.

ORDER FORM

Books in this series are available at your local bookshop, or can be ordered direct from the publisher. A complete list of titles is given on the previous page. Just tick the titles you would like and complete the details below. Prices and availability are subject to change without prior notice.

Please enclose a cheque or postal order made payable to Bookpoint Ltd, and send to: Hodder Children's Books, Cash Sales Dept, Bookpoint, 130 Milton Park, Abingdon, Oxon OX14 4SB. Email address: orders@bookpoint.co.uk.

If you would prefer to pay by credit card, our call centre team would be delighted to take your order by telephone. Our direct line is 01235 400400 (lines open 9.00 am – 6.00 pm, Monday to Saturday; 24 hour message answering service). Alternatively you can send a fax on 01235 400454.

Title .... First name .... Surname ....

Address...

....

....

Daytime tel .... Postcode ....

If you would prefer to post a credit card order, please complete the following.

Please debit my Visa/Access/Diners Card/American Express (delete as applicable) card number:

Signature .... Expiry Date ....
If you would NOT like to receive further information on our products, please tick ☐.